BULIMIA

Other books in the At Issue series:

Alcohol Abuse
Animal Experimentation
Anorexia
The Attack on America: September 11, 2001
Biological and Chemical Weapons
The Central Intelligence Agency
Cloning
Creationism vs. Evolution
Does Capital Punishment Deter Crime?
Drugs and Sports
Drunk Driving
The Ethics of Abortion
The Ethics of Genetic Engineering
The Ethics of Human Cloning
Heroin
Home Schooling
How Can Gun Violence Be Reduced?
How Should Prisons Treat Inmates?
Human Embryo Experimentation
Is Global Warming a Threat?
Islamic Fundamentalism
Is Media Violence a Problem?
Legalizing Drugs
Missile Defense
National Security
Nuclear and Toxic Waste
Nuclear Security
Organ Transplants
Performance-Enhancing Drugs
Physician-Assisted Suicide
Police Corruption
Professional Wrestling
Rain Forests
Satanism
School Shootings
Should Abortion Rights Be Restricted?
Should There Be Limits to Free Speech?
Teen Sex
Video Games
What Encourages Gang Behavior?
What Is a Hate Crime?
White Supremacy Groups

BULIMIA

Loreta M. Medina, *Book Editor*

Daniel Leone, *President*
Bonnie Szumski, *Publisher*
Scott Barbour, *Managing Editor*

GREENHAVEN
PRESS ®

GALE

San Diego • Detroit • New York • San Francisco • Cleveland
New Haven, Conn. • Waterville, Maine • London • Munich

For more information, contact
Greenhaven Press
27500 Drake Rd.
Farmington Hills, MI 48331-3535
Or you can visit our Internet site at http://www.gale.com

LIBRARY OF CONGRESS CATALOGING-IN-PUBLICATION DATA

Bulimia / Loreta M. Medina, book editor.
    p. cm. — (At issue)
Includes bibliographical references and index.
ISBN 0-7377-1164-7 (alk. paper) — ISBN 0-7377-1163-9 (pbk. : alk. paper)
    1. Bulimia. I. Medina, Loreta M. II. At issue (San Diego, Calif.)
RC552.B84 B84 2003
616.85'263—dc21   2002069733

Printed in the United States of America

Contents

Page

Introduction   6

1. Bulimia Nervosa: An Overview   10
   Beth M. McGilley and Tamara L. Pryor

2. Testimony of a Recovered Female Bulimic   17
   Sandy Fertman

3. Bulimia in Older Women   23
   Susan Chollar

4. Men Are Becoming More Vulnerable to Bulimia   28
   Lisa Liddane

5. Adolescence: Setting the Stage for Eating Disorders   32
   Marlene Boskind-White and William C. White Jr.

6. Bulimia May Be Linked to Sexual Abuse   40
   Jennifer Redford

7. Bingeing and Dieting as Methods of Coping with Pain   46
   Becky W. Thompson

8. Bulimia Is on the Rise Among Nonwhite Populations   54
   Kathryn J. Zerbe

9. Current Approaches to Treating Bulimia   60
   Carolyn Costin

10. The Role of Parents in a Child's Recovery   67
    Abigail H. Natenshon

Organizations to Contact   71

Bibliography   75

Index   77

Introduction

In recent years the incidence of bulimia in the United States has increased: The American Psychiatric Association estimates that today 1.1 to 4.2 percent of females will have bulimia in their lifetime. Many health professionals have expressed concern that bulimia, together with anorexia, binge eating, and other eating disorders may soon reach epidemic proportions. The Washington-based National Eating Disorders Association, which claims to be the largest advocacy and prevention organization in the world, estimates that 5 to 10 million girls and women and 1 million boys and men are battling some form of eating disorder in the United States.

Of those suffering from bulimia in the country, 90 to 95 percent are female. Most troubled are college-age women, teens, middle-aged women, and more recently, children. Among men, the most vulnerable are athletes, fitness enthusiasts, and those who have experienced various kinds of abuse, causing them to succumb to anxiety and, oftentimes, low self-esteem.

The fourth edition of the *American Psychiatric Association: Diagnostic and Statistical Manual of Mental Disorders,* published in 1994, defines bulimia as an eating disorder that involves episodes of binge eating and purging and lack of control over eating. To avoid gaining weight from huge food intakes, a bulimic person engages in self-induced vomiting and often misuses laxatives, diuretics, enemas, or other medications. He or she may also engage in fasting and compulsive exercise. The binge eating and the compensatory behavior occur at least twice a week for three months. Bulimics generally have normal body weights, but they are never satisfied with them. Having an ideal weight in mind, their overriding goal is to become thinner.

Bulimics usually binge on high-calorie junk foods like fast food, ice cream, french fries, sweets, and cookies, with calorie intake per binge running from one thousand to twenty thousand—way over the standard. One school of thought suggests that bulimia occurs more in developed countries because of higher intakes of processed carbohydrates. In contrast, developing and poorer countries mostly rely on whole grains and vegetables, which are always more healthful.

Most of a bulimic's routine is spent in finding the time and place to indulge in his or her uncontrollable habit. The person caught up in the disorder follows the cycle of bingeing and purging at home, at work, in a college dorm, at parties, during the day, and at night. The bulimic often feels shame, loneliness, isolation, guilt, and terror but finds it hard to break the cycle of eating and disgorging, eating and fasting, eating and laxatives, eating and compulsive exercise. The habit can even lead the individual to periodic lying and, in many cases, stealing; after all, mounds of food could cost a lot of money. Avoiding social activities, the bulimic rarely has meaningful friendships and intimate relationships.

The initial signs and symptoms of bulimia are sometimes misleading: vomiting, diarrhea, scarring of the fingers and hands, constipation, and menstrual irregularities. Often, this delays proper detection, which brings further harm to a suffering individual. Many health providers also note that many sufferers tend to deny the symptoms of the disorder. Repeated vomiting could lead to erosion of tooth enamel, dehydration, stomach ulcers, and eventually an imbalance in electrolytes, which could be life-threatening. Serious consequences include kidney damage, ruptured stomach or esophagus, irregular heartbeat, and seizures. Finally, bulimia can cause death from a damaged heart or loss of body chemicals. Author Debbie Stanley observes in her book *Understanding Bulimia Nervosa* that together with other eating disorders, bulimia and its twin, anorexia (which involves avoiding food to the point of starvation), account for more deaths than any other psychiatric condition.

Indeed, while its manifestations are physical, bulimia—again, like anorexia—is a mental disorder. A bulimic person suffers from abnormally low self-esteem, a desire for perfection, heightened loneliness and isolation, and an obsession with food. He or she is also prone to depression and anxiety. A bulimic shares several similarities with an anorexic: an obsession with diet, a distorted body image, a lack of self-esteem, and a sense of inadequacy. Both are likely young women who come from middle-class families with dominant mothers and uninvolved fathers. Hungry for approval, both bulimics and anorexics tend to become "dutiful daughters" and comply with family rules. Yet whereas an anorexic avoids food and is always starved, a bulimic is always on a cycle of bingeing and purging. A bulimic is also capable of a social and work life while an anorexic often is not.

The causes of bulimia in women—like anorexia and other eating disorders for that matter—have been initially attributed to a culture that stresses and rewards female thinness as well as to the mass media, which promote irrational standards of beauty. The Harvard Eating Disorders Center (HEDC) cites a study of children aged eight to ten wherein half of the girls and one-third of the boys reported being dissatisfied with their body size. The most dissatisfied among the girls wanted to be thinner, and the dissatisfied boys wanted to be heavier. Another study showed that expectations regarding thinness among young girls are evident as early as six and seven years old. In terms of actual dieting, HEDC cites a study of 457 fourth graders in which 40 percent reported dieting "very often" or "sometimes." Another study on dieting indicated that 31 to 46 percent of nine-year-olds and 46 to 81 percent of ten-year-olds reported dieting, fear of fatness, and binge eating.

It is disturbing that eating disorders may soon be afflicting more and more children and teens, and recent research on the nature of eating disorders does not offer relief either. Most studies point out that eating disorders are much more complex than a simple obsession with weight expressed in the misuse of food. Often the disorder is a mask for—if not a response to—deeper, far more serious psychological pathologies. Various research surveys have found sufferers to be dealing painfully with issues of self-worth, dysfunctional family relationships, unresolved conflicts, and traumatic childhood experiences. In many ways, bulimia is a coping mechanism employed during times of duress. Jennifer Redford, writing in

Physician Assistant in March 2001, cites numerous studies that link bulimia and sexual abuse in childhood.

Initially, studies have pointed to the most vulnerable group as young white middle-class women who are inclined toward traditional values such as successful careers and marriage. Marlene Boskind-White, a professional counselor who has helped thousands of bulimia sufferers on college campuses, observes that bulimic women are often attractive, bright, talented, and have potential for creative activity such as writing, dancing, painting, and acting. Also, they are able to pursue careers and often become over-achievers. In *Bulimia Anorexia: The Binge/Purge Cycle and Self-Starvation,* Boskind-White and coauthor William C. White Jr. explain the sufferer's drive as a compensation for her shortcomings. Based on their practice, the two authors note that a bulimic's pursuit of success is not for the joy of achievement but for the expected rewards, particularly from men.

More recent research shows that sufferers are no longer confined to the white middle-class female population. Growing evidence suggests that bulimia among non-Caucasians—including Native Americans, Hispanics, African Americans, and Asians—is on the rise. Kathryn Zerbe, a psychoanalyst and a former faculty member at the Karl Menninger School of Psychiatry, attributes this to the aforementioned groups' improved socioeconomic conditions, exposure to media stereotypes, and, more importantly, their vulnerability to destabilizing life change such as immigration, acculturation, and westernization.

Merry N. Miller and Andres J. Pumariega, both professors of the department of psychiatry at the James H. Quillen College of Medicine, Eastern Tennessee State University, echo the link between bulimia and sociocultural change. Writing in *Psychiatry* in the summer of 2001, they note that eating disorders such as bulimia occur when traditional ideas of physical attractiveness are threatened and supplanted with something else. The two authors also identify the changing role of women as a major factor. Supporting this contention, Karin Kratina, a dietician and consultant for Renfrew Center, which treats eating disorders, is quoted by Jim McCaffree in the *Journal of the American Dietetic Association* as saying, "Cultures that experience oppression of women in conjunction with increased expectations of women tend to have more incidences of eating disorders."

Becky Thompson, a sociologist and author, refutes the common contention that eating disorders are about women's vanity. Through in-depth interviews with a group composed of African Americans, Hispanics, and lesbians, she found that women resorted to eating disorders as a way of dealing with poverty, racism, alienation, sexism, and sexual abuse. Regarding the alienation that some groups may be experiencing, the HDEC cites a study involving 135 males with eating disorders that indicated that 42 percent of those diagnosed as bulimic were either gay or bisexual.

Another group that has been succumbing recently to eating disorders in bigger numbers is immigrant girls and women. Quoted in the March 6, 2000, issue of the *Washington Post*, Catherine Steiner-Adair of Harvard University's Eating Disorder Center says that one-fourth of her clients have been American teenagers whose parents were born in Latin America, Africa, the Middle East, and Asia. In their desire to blend into their communities, these women may be trying too hard to fit into the American ideal of thinness. To respond to the phenomenon, youth centers in places like Los Angeles and New York have started support groups for immigrants.

Acknowledging that eating disorders are, for the most part, a social problem, scholars like Miller and Pumariega propose that care providers should offer more carefully crafted programs of prevention and treatment. They stress that strategies have to strengthen personal identity, reach out more strongly to women of color and other disenfranchised groups, promote rational ideals of beauty, and reinforce adaptive practices. A meaningful program would also require clinicians to work across cultural differences and include the influence of traditional beliefs in their interventions.

While modes of treatment continue to evolve with the recognition that eating disorders are both medical and psychiatric concerns, researchers continue to unravel new information. A recent study in Britain found that bulimia springs partly from a deficiency in tryptophan, a chemical in the brain. Tryptophan, an amino acid that occurs naturally in many foods, is used by the body to make serotonin, which in turn regulates mood and appetite. In a 1999 *New York Times* article, lead researcher Katharine A. Smith of Oxford University said that the finding suggests that "lowered brain serotonin function can trigger some of the clinical features of bulimia nervosa in individuals vulnerable to the disorder." (In the same manner, anorexia nervosa is being studied on its possible link to a gene. The Eating Disorder Program of the University of Pittsburgh Medical Center Health Systems is participating in an international study that seeks to determine whether a gene or a set of genes might predispose individuals to develop anorexia nervosa.)

As eating disorders continue to spark more attention, as new research sheds new light on their nature, and as professionals continue to search for effective strategies for prevention, advocacy, and treatment, a better understanding of the issue may emerge, resulting in positive responses from various sectors. When this happens, more suffering individuals may come forward and seek help. Hopefully, millions of suffering women, children, and men—not to mention their families and communities—will be able to find solace and relief.

1

Bulimia Nervosa: An Overview

Beth M. McGilley and Tamara L. Pryor

Beth M. McGilley and Tamara L. Pryor codirect the eating disorder clinic at the University of Kansas School of Medicine in Wichita, where they are both faculty members. Beth M. McGilley maintains a private practice. Tamara L. Pryor is clinical associate professor in the Department of Psychiatry and Behavioral Sciences and a member of the Managed Care Task Force of the Academy of Eating Disorders.

Bulimia nervosa, more popularly known as bulimia, afflicts three percent of young women in the United States. It is considered a mental or psychiatric disorder with physical manifestations that include episodes of eating binges, followed by purging to prevent weight gain. It is also often accompanied by fasting, excessive exercise, and the misuse of diuretics, laxatives, or enemas. In severe cases, a victim may suffer from dental erosion, swollen salivary glands, gastrointestinal irritation, and loss of body fluids. Sufferers of this illness should be referred to a mental health professional with specific expertise in eating disorders. By evaluating a patient's medical condition, attitudes and behaviors, developmental history, and interpersonal relationships, a professional can determine the most appropriate treatment for the patient.

Bulimia nervosa is a psychiatric syndrome with potentially serious consequences. Relatively effective treatments for this disorder have been developed, and early intervention is more likely to facilitate eventual recovery. Unfortunately, few health care professionals receive training in the assessment of bulimia nervosa. Therefore, they may be unable to identify and treat patients with the disorder.

Historically, patients with bulimia nervosa often were hospitalized until the most disruptive symptoms ceased. In today's health care environment, hospitalization for bulimia nervosa is infrequent and tends to take the form of brief admissions focused on crisis management. Specialists in the field of eating disorders have responded to the present cost-containment measures by developing a combination of treatment modalities, including medication and individual and group psychotherapy, that can be used in the outpatient care of patients with bulimia nervosa. This article discusses the assessment and treatment of bulimia nervosa and considers how this disorder can best be handled in a managed care environment.

Bulimia nervosa is a multifaceted disorder with psychologic, physiologic, developmental and cultural components. There may be a genetic predisposition for the disorder. Other predisposing factors include psychologic and personality factors, such as perfectionism, impaired self-concept, affective instability, poor impulse control and an absence of adaptive functioning to maturational tasks and developmental stressors (e.g., puberty; peer and parental relationships, sexuality, marriage and pregnancy).

Bulimia nervosa is a multifaceted disorder with psychologic, physiologic, developmental and cultural components.

Biologic researchers suggest that abnormalities of central nervous system neurotransmitters may also play a role in bulimia nervosa. Furthermore, several familial factors may increase the risk of developing this disorder. For example, researchers have discovered that first- and second-degree relatives of individuals with bulimia nervosa have an increased incidence of depression and manic-depressive illnesses, eating disorders, and alcohol and substance abuse problems.

Regardless of the cause, once bulimia nervosa is present, the physiologic effects of disordered eating appear to maintain the core features of the disorder, resulting in a self-perpetuating cycle.

Diagnosing bulimia

The diagnostic criteria for bulimia nervosa (Table 1) now include subtypes to distinguish patients who compensate for binge eating by purging (vomiting and/or the abuse of laxatives and diuretics) from those who use nonpurging behaviors (e.g., fasting or excessive exercising).

A binge eating/purging subtype of anorexia nervosa also exists. Low body weight is the major factor that differentiates bulimia nervosa from this subtype of anorexia nervosa. Thus, according to the established diagnostic criteria, patients who are 15 percent below natural bodyweight and binge eat or purge are considered to have anorexia nervosa. Patients can, and frequently do, move between diagnostic categories as their symptom pattern and weight change over the course of the illness.

Some patients do not meet the full criteria for bulimia nervosa or anorexia nervosa. These patients may be classified as having an eating disorder "not otherwise specified.". . .

Prevalence of bulimia

Bulimia nervosa appears to have become more prevalent during the past 30 years. The disorder is 10 times more common in females than in males

Table 1: Diagnostic Criteria for Bulimia Nervosa

A. Recurrent episodes of binge eating. An episode of binge eating is characterized by both of the following:
  1. Eating, in a discrete period of time (e.g., within a two-hour period), an amount of food that is definitely larger than most people would eat during a similar period of time and under similar circumstances.
  2. A sense of lack of control over eating during the episode (e.g., a feeling that one cannot stop eating or control what or how much one is eating).

B. Recurrent inappropriate compensatory behavior in order to prevent weight gain, such as self-induced vomiting; misuse of laxatives, diuretics, enemas, or other medications; fasting or excessive exercise.

C. The binge eating and inappropriate compensatory behaviors both occur, on average, at least twice a week for three months.

D. Self-evaluation is unduly influenced by body shape and weight.

E. The disturbance does not occur exclusively during episodes of anorexia nervosa.

Specific types:
• Purging type: during the current episode of bulimia nervosa, the person has regularly engaged in self-induced vomiting or the misuse of laxatives, diuretics, or enemas.
• Nonpurging type: during the current episode of bulimia nervosa, the person has used other inappropriate compensatory behaviors, such as fasting or excessive exercise, but has not regularly engaged in self-induced vomiting or the misuse of laxatives, diuretics, or enemas.

Reprinted with permission from American Psychiatric Association. Diagnostic and statistical manual of mental disorders. 4th ed. Washington, D.C.: American Psychiatric Association, 1994: 549–50.

and affects 1 to 3 percent of female adolescents and young adults.

Both anorexia nervosa and bulimia nervosa have a peak onset between the ages of 13 and 20 years. The disorder appears to have a chronic, sometimes episodic course in which periods of remission alternate with recurrences of binge/purge cycles. Some patients have bulimia nervosa that persists for 30 years or more. Recent data suggest that patients with subsyndromal bulimia nervosa may show morbidity comparable to that in patients with the full syndrome.

The long-term outcome of bulimia nervosa is not known. Available research indicates that 30 percent of patients with bulimia nervosa rapidly relapse and up to 40 percent remain chronically symptomatic.

Psychiatric conditions related to bulimia

Clinical and research reports emphasize a frequent association between bulimia nervosa and other psychiatric conditions. Comorbid major depression is commonly noted (Table 2), although it is not clear if the mood disturbance is a function of bulimia nervosa or a separate phenomenon.

Table 2: Psychiatric Conditions Commonly Coexisting with Bulimia Nervosa

• Mood disorders: major depression, dysthymic disorder, and bipolar disorder.

• Substance-related disorders: alcohol abuse, stimulant abuse, and polysubstance abuse.

• Anxiety disorders: panic disorder, obsessive-compulsive disorder, generalized anxiety disorder, and post-traumatic stress disorder.

• Personality disorders: borderline personality disorder, histrionic personality disorder, narcissistic personality disorder, and antisocial personality disorder.

Information concerning the comorbidity rates of bipolar disorders (e.g., manic depression, rapid cycling mood disorder) and bulimia nervosa is somewhat limited. However, recent epidemiologic data indicate an increased incidence of rapid cycling mood disorders in patients with more severe, chronic bulimia nervosa.

The association between bulimia nervosa and other anxiety and substance-related disorders has been well documented. For example, substance abuse or dependence, particularly involving alcohol and stimulants, occurs in one third of patients with bulimia nervosa. Thus, a comorbid substance-related disorder must be addressed before effective treatment for bulimia nervosa can be initiated.

Significant research has been devoted to the high frequency of personality disturbances in patients with bulimia nervosa. Overall, between 2 and 50 percent of women with bulimia nervosa have some type of personality disorder, most commonly borderline, antisocial, histrionic or narcissistic personality disorder.

To ensure that the treatment approach is properly designed and effective, the physician must look carefully for symptoms of comorbid psychiatric illness in patients with bulimia nervosa. Although further research is needed to determine the extent to which comorbid conditions influence the course of bulimia nervosa, the presence of these additional problems clearly complicates the treatment process.

Medical complications

The medical complications of bulimia nervosa range from fairly benign, transient symptoms, such as fatigue, bloating and constipation, to chronic or life-threatening conditions, including hypokalemia, cathartic colon, impaired renal function and cardiac arrest. . . .

Binge eating alone rarely causes significant medical complications. Gastric rupture, the most serious complication, is uncommon. More often, patients describe nausea, abdominal pain and distention, prolonged digestion and weight gain.

The combination of heightened anxiety, physical discomfort and intense guilt provokes the drive to purge the food by self-induced vomiting, excessive exercise or the misuse of ipecac, laxatives or diuretics. These purgative methods are associated with the more serious complications of bulimia nervosa.

Self-induced vomiting

Self-induced vomiting, the most common means of purging, is used by more than 75 percent of patients with bulimia nervosa. Most patients vomit immediately or soon after a binge. During the binge, they commonly drink excessive fluids to "float the food" and facilitate regurgitation.

Bulimia nervosa appears to have become more prevalent during the past 30 years.

Vomiting is induced by stimulation of the pharynx using a finger or a narrow object such as a toothbrush. Some patients describe the learned ability to vomit by pressure or contraction of the abdominal muscles. A minority of patients develop reflux following the consumption of virtually any amount of food or fluid. Treatment of this reflux is difficult and requires that the patient practice relaxation during food ingestion.

Self-induced vomiting can lead to a number of serious medical complications.

- Dental Erosion. Gastric acids may cause deterioration of tooth enamel (perimolysis), particularly involving the occlusal surfaces of molars and the posterior surfaces of maxillary incisors. Since these effects are irreversible, patients with this complication need to have regular dental care.
- Enlarged Salivary Glands. Frequent vomiting has been reported to cause swelling of the salivary glands in approximately 8 percent of patients with bulimia nervosa. The exact etiology is unknown. The glandular enlargement is typically painless and may occur within several days of excessive vomiting. It appears to be a cosmetically distressing but medically benign condition. Other than cessation of vomiting, no specific treatment has been identified.
- Oral and Hand Trauma. The induction of vomiting with a finger or an object can cause lacerations of the mouth and throat. Bleeding lacerations can also occur on the knuckles because of repeated contact with the front teeth. Some patients with bulimia nervosa develop a calloused, scarred area distal to their knuckles. Oral or hand trauma can provide evidence of vomiting even when patients deny bulimic symptoms.
- Esophageal and Pharyngeal Complications. Because of repeated contact with gastric acids, the esophagus or pharynx may become irritated. Heartburn and sore throats may occur and are best treated with antacids and throat lozenges, respectively.

- Blood in the vomitus is an indication of upper gastrointestinal tears, which are a more serious complication of purging. Most tears heal well with cessation of vomiting. Perforation of the upper digestive tract, esophagus or stomach is an extremely rare but potentially lethal complication. Patients with gastric pain and excessive blood in their vomitus should be evaluated on an urgent basis.
- Electrolyte Imbalances. Serious depletions of hydrogen chloride, potassium, sodium and magnesium can occur because of the excessive loss of fluids during vomiting. Hypokalemia represents a potential medical emergency, and serum electrolyte levels should be measured as part of the initial evaluation in all new patients. Patients who complain of fatigue, muscle spasms or heart palpitations may be experiencing transient episodes of electrolyte disturbance. Paresthesias, tetany, seizures or cardiac arrhythmias are potential metabolic complications that require acute care. Chemistry profiles should be obtained regularly in patients who continue to vomit or abuse purgatives on a regular basis.

Assessment and treatment

Since bulimia nervosa has numerous medical complications, a complete physical examination is imperative in patients with this disorder. The examination should include vital signs and an evaluation of height and weight relative to age. The physician should also look for general hair loss, lanugo, abdominal tenderness, acrocyanosis (cyanosis of the extremities), jaundice, edema, parotid gland tenderness or enlargement, and scars on the dorsum of the hand.

Routine laboratory tests in patients with bulimia nervosa include a complete blood count with differential, serum chemistry and thyroid profiles, and urine chemistry microscopy testing. Depending on the results of the physical examination, additional laboratory tests, such as a chest radiograph and an electrocardiogram, may be indicated. Finally, patients who engage in self-induced vomiting should be referred for a complete dental examination.

Between 2 and 50 percent of women with bulimia nervosa have some type of personality disorder.

Because of the multifaceted nature of bulimia nervosa, a comprehensive psychiatric assessment is essential to developing the most appropriate treatment strategy. Patients should be referred to a mental health professional with specific expertise in this area. Frequently, student health programs or university medical centers have personnel who are experienced in the evaluation and treatment of eating disorders. . . .

The most appropriate course of treatment can usually be determined on the basis of a thorough evaluation of the patient's medical condition, associated eating behaviors and attitudes, body image, personality, developmental history and interpersonal relationships.

In the present managed care environment, hospitalization for patients with bulimia nervosa is no longer readily available. It has become especially important to determine a treatment approach that will be effective as quickly as possible. The physician needs to know when inpatient treatment is or is not indicated. A comprehensive evaluation provides the rationale for this judgment and includes the following:

1. Standardized testing to document the patient's general personality features, characterologic disturbance and attitudes about eating, body size and weight.

2. A complete history of the patient's body weight, eating patterns and attempts at weight loss, including typical daily food intake, methods of purging and perceived ideal weight.

3. An investigation of the patient's interpersonal history and functioning, including family dynamics, peer relationships, and present or past physical, sexual or emotional abuse.

4. An evaluation of medical and psychiatric comorbidity, as well as documentation of previous attempts at treatment.

Considerable research has been devoted to identifying the most effective pharmacologic and psychologic treatments for bulimia nervosa, including the effects of different medications (e.g., tricyclic antidepressants and selective serotonin reuptake inhibitors) and the benefits of different psychotherapy approaches (e.g., behavioral treatment versus cognitive-behavioral therapy and individual versus group therapies). In addition, a few studies have compared the efficacies of different combinations of medications and psychotherapy.

2

Testimony of a Recovered Female Bulimic

Sandy Fertman

Sandy Fertman contributes to Teen Magazine, *from which this article is taken.*

The author relates the story of an anonymous recovered bulimic whom she calls Kelly. Kelly's bout with bulimia started when she was a teen. Eating, bingeing, and disgorging were her ways of compensating for her lack of self-esteem. On one particular occasion, she suffered a massive loss of body liquid, and as a result Kelly had a heart attack. After hospitalization, Kelly started to seek professional help. However, it was not until her third heart attack that she decided finally to stop. Looking back to the traumatic years, Kelly now says battling bulimia is the bravest thing she has ever done.

You'd think Kelly* had it all. She's pretty, outgoing and smart. Who'd guess that all through high school, she was addicted to food, eating large quantities and then throwing up . . . until it almost cost her her life. In her own words, Kelly shares her lonely and humiliating tale and tells us how she's finally kicked this dangerous disease.

Kelly's story

I guess I'd say l had a pretty normal childhood.

I grew up in a house in California with my older brother, Jackson, and my identical twin sister, Carey. My sister and I have always been really close, but it's hard not to be when you're identical twins. My father is a psychologist and my mom owns a travel agency, but they were separated when I was about five. Carey, Jackson and I lived with our mom. Still, my dad has always been very much a part of my life.

My mom has always been overweight. I think her fears of us getting

---

* The names used in this article have been changed.

fat were instilled in us, even though she never voiced them. I first became aware of my own weight when I was around 15. One day, I looked in the mirror and noticed my face was changing. It looked kind of heavy and I thought, "Oh, my God! I have to lose weight!" It just hit me like a punch in the stomach.

From age seven, I had been a gymnast. I wasn't thin, but I always had to be aware of my body. But by the time I was 15, I was also modeling and acting, so I really had to start watching my weight.

I felt a sense of power after that first time I purged. I thought I felt great that first night.

I had this diet of eating only steamed vegetables. One night, I ate too many vegetables and felt really sick. My mom said, "Oh, Kelly, just throw up." I said, "No way! That's so disgusting!" Mom said, calmly, "Just do it, Kelly. You'll feel better." She told me to just stick my finger down my throat. So I did and after that, it became a habit, a really long, bad habit.

I felt a sense of power after that first time I purged. I thought I felt great that first night.

Both my sister and I learned how to purge that way. Carey and I would even throw up at the same time! We didn't think there was anything wrong with it. My mom knew the first couple of times, but then we decided we'd keep it our secret.

That secret lasted five years. I thought I'd kept it a secret from my friends, but later I found out they all knew. Your friends always know. They see how much you eat and you think you're being sneaky, saying you exercise a lot or that you have a fast metabolism. But after you come out of the bathroom and your face is all puffy, your eyes watery and your nose runny, they know what's going on. They just didn't have a clue what to do about it.

Living a lie

My sister and I didn't really talk about our purging, but we both understood that if we ate a lot at any meal, we'd both have to sneak out and 'get rid of it.' After dinner at home, I'd usually run a bath to disguise the noise of vomiting. If I couldn't find a bathroom, I'd drive somewhere and get rid of it—in a bathroom, the bushes, wherever. At parties, I'd just 'get sick' in the bathroom after eating a lot of snacks. I usually could do it faster than someone could go to the bathroom! I'd eat until I was uncomfortable and then just go get rid of it.

My problem began to take total control of my life, because all I did all the time was try to figure out ways to eat a lot and how I was going to get rid of it. That's what your entire life is about. You make sure you won't even get into a situation where you can't throw up. So you end up planning your life around your eating and vomiting and it ends up controlling you. I avoided all camping trips, boat trips, excursions, even sleeping over at friends' houses just so I could eat and purge. It's a nightmare. You constantly have to sneak around, change your plans, lie. I'd plan ahead all of my excuses to allow me to stay in the bathroom when I went out to dinner with friends, making up things like, "There was a long line" or quickly slapping on some lipstick and saying, "Oh, I just had to retouch my makeup." You're always lying. It's sick.

I hardly ever ate fatty foods, because I was still watching my weight, but a few times a week I'd say, "Well, I can eat anything I want!" so I'd eat a donut or two and then purge. I got a lot of attention from being thin and at the time, that made it all worth it to me. In fact, most bulimic girls are never obese; they're usually average in weight, but want to have that 'edge' over other girls. I felt inferior to everyone else, so I'd think, 'If I can only have control over this one thing, I'll be able to make up for all my deficiencies.'

Obviously, I didn't have much of a sense of self-worth and truly didn't like myself a lot, never thinking I was smart enough, pretty enough or funny enough. You feel like you're not worthy of being loved or even liked. So you get into this self-destructive behavior, thinking that if you're thin, it will compensate for all your inadequacies. But even though you think you've got it under control, you're way out of control!

Feeling like a fraud

The worst feeling was that I felt like a fraud all the time, always keeping this secret, hiding this habit. I was so ashamed. It's such a secret that your whole life becomes centered around keeping it. I chose friends that could never get close to me, because if they did, they'd figure out my little secret. In my case, though, I was lucky to still have my childhood friends, but the people I really began to hang out with were very emotionally detached and distant people. That's what I wanted.

My problem began to take total control of my life, because all I did all the time was try to figure out ways to eat a lot and how I was going to get rid of it.

During the whole time I was eating and purging, I never had a boyfriend. I didn't feel lovable; I figured no one would want me. I dated a lot, but even to this day, I haven't gotten serious with anyone. I was very social, but it was always very superficial, like going to dances and hanging out with large groups of friends, nothing intimate. It was really easy to hide my problem from the guys I dated, because no one assumes you're going to the bathroom to vomit. . . .

I was always faking it, always full of lies and excuses to enable me to keep my secret. I'd say to my friends, "Oh, I've gotta get going" or "I've gotta run some errands," nonspecific excuses so I could go munch out and throw up. Your life revolves around eating. It got to a point where I didn't need to use my finger or anything. My muscles just did it.

Lying all the time made me feel terrible about myself. I knew I had a serious problem if l had to deceive people all the time to keep it up. You realize you're trapped, but it's literally the most important thing in your life. My best friend knew about it; in fact, all my closest friends did and they'd talk to me about it, but they couldn't change me. Sometimes they'd just walk away, but since they're friends for life, they eventually came back. In that way, I was incredibly fortunate.

Eating me up inside

I was always an A student, but during my senior year, I got kicked out of high school. I simply lost interest in school and everything about it. I was just so bored and I had started hanging out with this group of friends outside of school who I called, the low-lifes. I just didn't care about anything anymore, except my habit, of course.

Things went from bad to worse that year. By then, I was throwing up six times a day, every day. One afternoon, I was sitting in traffic school and I suddenly got this tingling feeling in my hands and then my muscles started contracting and curling up and contorting. My whole body just froze! I excused myself and went to the pay phone to get help and when I started walking back, I screamed, "Oh, my God!!" and I collapsed on the floor by the classroom—my legs were paralyzed. I couldn't move any of my muscles, even my tongue! My mom came to get me and said we'd wait until the morning to see how I felt. I said, "Mom, I may not be alive in the morning!" so she drove straight to the emergency room.

The doctor examining me told us I had had a minor heart attack. He explained that I had hardly any electrolytes left in my body from throwing up so much. Those minerals maintain your heart and muscle activity, basically everything. My mom, of course, had known I was bulimic, but now she, too, had to face up to it. The nurses immediately injected my vein with a needle and hooked me up to this potassium drip. It was the worst pain I have ever felt in my life, like razor blades going through every vein in my body! You can feel it going into your arms, your shoulders, your heart, your stomach, your thighs, your legs and your feet. It's like someone is taking razor blades soaked in salt and alcohol and dragging them slowly through your body. I was crying through the whole procedure, "Please stop it! Please, please!" But it was either that or I'd die. . . .

I stayed overnight in the hospital and you'd think I would have learned my lesson, but l didn't. I started throwing up right afterward. I felt like the alternative to purging was getting fat and I really believed that was worse than having a heart attack!

Everyone told me I had to see a therapist, so I went to a counseling group at the local university medical center for a short time.

Friends to the rescue

My true friends decided it was time to take action, so they did an 'intervention.' That's when your friends and family get together and confront you all at once with your problem. My sister and four friends showed up at my house and all day long they kept saying, "Kelly, you're so smart and so beautiful, you don't need to do this!" They said they just didn't understand how I could do this to myself, basically letting me know how much it was hurting them. I felt like I was really disappointing them, like something was really abnormal about me. That's what really made me feel like

I had to do something about my bulimia; I felt so incredibly ashamed.

The intervention was actually wonderful because my secret was finally lifted off of my shoulders. As painful as it was to be told I was, in a way, a failure, it was good for me. I realized I needed help.

At that time, I looked so strange because of my problem. My face became a 'moon face'—kind of puffy and round which is pretty common with bulimics, my teeth had decayed from the acids of regurgitating, my eyes were kind of filmy and my hair had started falling out. Starting to eat normally again was incredibly hard. It was hard to start digesting again. You almost have to eat all liquids at first. I started swelling so badly for about 24 hours after eating that the doctors put me on a diuretic [that's a medication to get rid of the excess water] and other medications for digestion.

Make sure you talk to someone before it's too late. Bulimia can kill you.

After that intervention, I stopped purging. By that time, Carey was already going to group and individual counseling and was taking medication to treat her bulimia. I never did any of that. But only a year later, I started throwing up again. I hadn't broken the habit. I ended up having another minor heart attack while I was driving home from the gym one day. Even at the hospital while I was getting that horrible potassium drip, I was wondering, "How can I keep eating and getting rid of it without dying?" I can't believe that I was that out of control!

Just one week later, I was back in the hospital with another heart attack and that's when I thought, "Oh, my God! I can't control this!" That's when I decided to stop it for good.

Filling myself up

It's been three years now and I feel great. Although I've never gone to therapy, I do talk to another recovering bulimic about it. I knew I didn't want to die and I started realizing who I was and that I really did like myself.

I took the proficiency test to graduate from high school and then went on to graduate from the local university magna cum laude. Now I have my own television production company and I'm producing an outdoor-related TV series. I really love my work. Actually, most bulimics are very ambitious people. They're into that 'control thing' so they know what they want and are inspired to go to extremes to get it—not that that's always good.

My whole life has changed without the pressure of hiding a secret and supporting a habit. All of a sudden, you have an empty part of your life you have to fill. It's like when you end a relationship with a boyfriend: You've been seeing him and then all of a sudden he's not there anymore. That's what I'm doing now. Battling bulimia was the bravest thing I've ever done. Now I have to face those fears of 'getting big' and having no one like me. Today, I'm 15 pounds heavier than I was when I was bulimic, but I think I'm in good shape. And most importantly, I'm really happy.

Food for thought

If you're starting to binge and purge, you aren't in control just because you're controlling your weight. Actually, you're way out of control. Once you start purging, it's like cigarettes. It's a hard habit to break. It's with you for years, maybe even a lifetime. You think you can stop any time, but your fear of getting fat is so overwhelming that you're driven to this extreme behavior. And even if you think it's your little secret, it's not! You're not fooling anyone! People close to you know.

Definitely talk to someone about your feelings. Confide in your good friends. If you're close to your parents and you have an open relationship with them, talk to them. You can also go to a 12-step program, such as Overeaters Anonymous. Or you can go to an eating disorder clinic or see a therapist or a counselor. But make sure you talk to someone before it's too late. Bulimia can kill you. I know. It almost killed me.

3

Bulimia in Older Women

Susan Chollar

Susan Chollar writes for Woman's Day, *from which this article is taken.*

Often seen as an adolescent illness, bulimia is increasingly afflicting older women. Of the 8 million people who suffer from eating disorders, 90 percent are women and one out of every ten is over the age of twenty-five. Considering that eating disorders remain under-reported, the number could be higher. Bulimia—like its twin, anorexia nervosa—is often caused by a change in a woman's life like pregnancy, menopause, and personal crisis, as well as by common causes such as cultural norms, the family, and individual personality.

Many have endured years of silent shame, but now women in their 30s and older are confronting a problem that goes well beyond adolescence.

For 25 years Mary Jane Hamilton lived with a dark secret that filled her with self-disgust and distanced her from those she loved most. At age 17, plagued by anxiety, fear and loneliness, Mary Jane first developed anorexia nervosa, then, a year later, bulimia nervosa.

In a desperate effort to fill up an emptiness she was feeling inside, she would overeat and then force herself to vomit. "Food had such a wonderful way of numbing me out," recalls the 50-year-old from Kalamazoo, Michigan.

Mary Jane's experience with bulimia was not a passing phase. For most of her adult life—throughout her courtship, marriage and motherhood to two young children—she continued to binge and purge in secret. "No one ever suspected," she says. "I was so afraid of being discovered that I took on a very self-sufficient, tough-girl image that kept people at a distance." Finally, in her early 40s, when her children were nearly grown, she began to realize all that she had lost to her eating disorder. "The day my son left for college I wondered where all the time had gone," she recalls. "It seemed that food was always blocking the path to giving and receiving love."

Although the eating disorders bulimia nervosa and anorexia nervosa are often described as adolescent illnesses, health professionals are beginning to realize that there is a large and, some think, growing number of women in their 30s, 40s, 50s and beyond who also suffer. Some began their love/hate relationship with food in girlhood; others developed the obsession as adults. Each woman has her own tragic tale to tell—women like . . .

- Gail Thorpe, 34, who made it through a terrible childhood and an even worse adolescence, only to slip into anorexia as an adult, after she married and found the secure home that she had always wanted.
- Joelle Brady, 30, who had been bingeing and purging for half her life. She has been able to kick her alcohol habit but still struggles with food-related issues. Longing to have a child, she is determined to resolve her conflict over food before she gets pregnant.
- Sheri Glazier, who became anorexic at age 33, five years after the birth of her third child. She nearly died from the disease at age 41 when her weight dropped to 48 pounds.
- Adele Michaels,* 39, who has been borderline anorexic for her entire adult life. When her teenage daughter developed anorexia, Adele recognized that she, too, needed help.
- Virginia Adler,* who, at age 67, finally realized that her secret behavior had a name. She sought treatment for the bulimia that had haunted her for more than 50 years after reading a magazine article on eating disorders.

How widespread?

Approximately 8 million people in the United States—90 percent of them women—suffer from eating disorders, according to the National Association of Anorexia Nervosa and Associated Disorders (ANAD). A report by the National Institute of Mental Health estimates that about one out of every 10 victims is over the age of 25. "We don't have good statistics because these women can be so secretive," says Kathryn J. Zerbe, M.D., vice president for education and research at the Menninger Clinic in Topeka, Kansas, and author of *The Body Betrayed*. Many experts believe that the numbers are alarmingly high.

There is a large and, some think, growing number of women in their 30s, 40s, 50s and beyond who also suffer.

And the consequences of their destructive relationship to food can be devastating. Anorexics literally starve vital organs such as the brain, which can lead to personality changes, and the heart, which can lead to irregular heart rhythms or, in the worst case, heart failure. Bulimics who vomit regularly damage their teeth and esophagus, and those who abuse laxatives can end up with serious bowel problems.

Both anorexia and bulimia can cause irregular menstrual periods and infertility, and, because of prolonged inadequate nutrition, both disor-

* Not her real name

ders can rob the bones of calcium. "I have lost some teeth and I have advanced osteoporosis," says 33-year-old Holly Hartman, a full-time homemaker from Glenview, Illinois, who has been both anorexic and bulimic and who, at the height of her bulimia, vomited dozens of times each day. "These women may have a skeleton that looks like a 70-year-old woman by the age of 40," says Sharon A. Alger, M.D., an associate professor of medicine at Albany Medical College.

The causes of eating disorders

"Eating disorders are coping mechanisms," explains Nancy Head Thode, M.S.W., a senior family therapist at the Wilkins Center for Eating Disorders in Greenwich, Connecticut. "They may develop in response to some stress in a person's life. Adolescence and the college years, for example, are times of overwhelming stress," she says. If the eating disorder is not detected or treated effectively during those years, that teenage girl is likely to grow into a woman with an eating disorder.

Both anorexia and bulimia can cause irregular menstrual periods and infertility, and . . . both disorders can rob the bones of calcium.

Most experts believe that it takes multiple factors to set the behavior in motion. "It's like a big stew. You have to have a lot of ingredients," says Patricia Fallon, Ph.D., a psychologist and faculty member at the University of Washington, in Seattle. "Among them can be culture, the family, trauma, personality and, now it appears, a genetic predisposition."

An eating disorder often emerges during a period of change in a woman's life. "These are people who have difficulty dealing with transition," says Janet David, Ph.D., of the Center for the Study of Anorexia and Bulimia in New York City. "That is why you often see their problems developing at specific points in the life cycle." For example, pregnancy can be a daunting experience for a woman terrified of gaining weight, as is menopause and the bodily changes that often accompany it.

There are other, more subtle kinds of crises, too. "I was a mother who loved babies," says 45-year-old Dawn Ries, an office administrator who lives in Northbrook, Illinois, and who has run an eating disorders support group since her recovery from anorexia. "I had a great need to be needed, but as they got older they didn't need me as much. At 30, something just snapped. I had a good husband and four great kids, but I was not happy. I had an endless number of deep holes that no one seemed to be able to fill."

Along with the personal traumas, our cultural quest for thinness has contributed to eating disorders. "Close to 80 percent of all women in America are dieting but don't understand how really insidious it is," says psychotherapist Carol Bloom, C.S.W., cofounder of the Women's Therapy Centre Institute in New York City. "You feel frightened about food, you feel that your body is not complying with your wishes. Most people diet their way up to a larger body size and often into an eating problem."

The family suffers

"For women who have been struggling for years, their way of coping with stress permeates all of their life," says Dr. Alger. "It influences their relationships, their ability to interact with other people and the pleasure they can get from relationships."

"Close to 80 percent of all women in America are dieting but don't understand how really insidious it is."

Even the most well-concealed eating disorder takes a toll on a woman's family. "A mom struggling with bulimia may miss school activities or other important events because she is out scouting around for food or sleeping off a binge. And if she is bingeing or purging, she doesn't want the kids to know her shame," says psychotherapist Nancy King, L.C.S.W., of the Wilkins Center for Eating Disorders in Greenwich, Connecticut.

Also, some women inadvertently put their children at risk by passing on unhealthy messages about food. Joelle Brady's mother put her on her first diet at age 10. "We see many patients whose mothers have eating disorders even though they were never labeled as that," says King. "Many of these daughters were told they were fat, when they weren't. Many were told that the boys wouldn't like them if they were not skinny. Many watched Mom diet endlessly." Even the most well-intentioned mother with an eating disorder may lack perspective on how much food is appropriate. "I've seen women who have problems feeding their babies because they don't know how to regulate their own food intake and they don't trust their own bodies," says Dr. David.

Support during treatment

Many women suffer in silence for years because they become masters of deception and denial and because family, friends and a poorly informed medical community have failed to recognize their symptoms. For one thing, women who develop an eating disorder as adults may lack the support system that younger women have. "Almost all teens with anorexia nervosa are in treatment because someone forces them to be," says Katherine Halmi, M.D., director of the Eating Disorders Program at Cornell Medical Center–Westchester Division. "But you can't force adults. They are often socially withdrawn and frequently unmarried, so there is no one in their environment to help provide structure and support."

Even when they're fortunate enough to find treatment, adults are often tougher to treat than teens. Often, many women with long-term cases have another form of mental illness such as depression or a drug or alcohol addiction, all of which can confound the recovery process. "The course of the illness can be very erratic, very up-and-down," says Dr. David. "A woman might do well for a couple of years and then need to come back into treatment."

Some adults, however, are more open to therapy than their teenage counterparts. "Oftentimes they are in therapy because they want to be and that makes them eminently treatable," Dr. Fallon says. "They have already gone over a hurdle that with adolescents you have to work pretty hard to get over: They have moved from seeing their eating disorder as something that gets them what they want to seeing it as something that gets in the way, and that is an enormous shift," she says.

"I guess that for a long time I wanted to die," Gail Thorpe recalls. "I was so unhappy and had so much self-hate and sadness from my early life—it was a type of slow suicide. Then something changed inside of me—I'm not sure why—but I really wanted to get better and I was willing to do whatever it took."

With research and reporting by Lisa Rounds.

4

Men Are Becoming More Vulnerable to Bulimia

Lisa Liddane

Lisa Liddane writes for the Orange County Register *in California.*

Eating disorders, including bulimia, affect more women than men, but their prevalence among the male population is rising. A recent estimate suggests that 10 percent of the 8 million people suffering from eating disorders are male. A study conducted in 1999 claims one in six men may have anorexia and bulimia. The number could be greater, considering that men are less inclined to recognize they have health problems and seek medical intervention. The most vulnerable are those who have a distorted body-image and a history of obsessive behavior.

The secret signs of bulimia and anorexia are familiar. Looking in the mirror and always seeing an unfit, unattractive, fat person—even when the real reflection isn't. Purging in the restroom after eating dinner with friends. Starving oneself by eating only one meal a day. Thinking constantly about one's body.

But the person in the mirror is not familiar.

It's a man.

His name is Dick. The 32-year-old sales associate from Anaheim asked that his last name not be used. None of his family members, friends and co-workers knows that he has been struggling for more than a decade with a distorted body image.

Dick is among a growing number of men—about 1 million in the United States, by most estimates—who battle with what is still largely perceived as a woman's mental health condition. The numbers of men with eating disorders may be greater—from 3 million to 5 million, said Roberto Olivardia, clinical psychologist at McLean Hospital in Belmont, Mass. Olivardia is co-author of *The Adonis Complex: The Secret Crisis of Male Body Obsession.*

Male eating disorders are underdiagnosed because society lacks awareness of them and men are less likely to admit they have this medical problem and seek help, Olivardia said.

That's changing slowly, he said.

Knowing who might be at risk may help prevent eating disorders from developing, say body-image researchers. Understanding the nature of male body obsession and eating disorders may help men recognize that they have these conditions and seek treatment.

Research is on the rise

Doctors and psychologists do not know the exact causes of distorted body images and eating disorders in men because research in these areas is in the infancy stages.

But more studies on men and boys are emerging in medical publications such as the *International Journal of Eating Disorders Research.*

One in six men may have anorexia and bulimia, according to a 1999 study in *Psychiatric Annals,* by Dr. Arnold E. Andersen, an eating-disorder researcher at University of Iowa.

Andersen classifies at-risk men into four groups:
- Men in sports and athletic activities who need to control weight for performance. This is the most prevalent group.
- Men who were overweight or obese and had negative, sometimes traumatic experiences related to their weight.
- Men whose fathers had ill health, possibly weight-related, or may have died because of it.
- Men who want to improve their body image. This includes gay and straight men.

Researchers have coined a term for one type of male body obsession: body dysmorphia disorder (BDD). An example of BDD is muscle dysmorphia, sometimes called "reverse anorexia" or "biggerexia." This disorder occurs when normal-size or big, muscular men think of themselves as thin and scrawny. Some men with muscle dysmorphia may be workoutaholics, or users of steroids or muscle-enhancing supplements.

Researchers also know that the effects of eating disorders on men are similar to those on women: weakened, fragile bones, elevated risk for heart attacks because of electrolyte imbalance, tooth decay, gastrointestinal problems and damage to the esophagus.

One theory in research that is gaining ground is the genetic link. Scientists suspect that the predisposition to an eating disorder may run in some families and in both sexes.

Society is involved

But genes aren't the only factors to blame. In the past decade, magazines such as *Men's Health* have perpetuated the myth that the look of male health is lean, low in fat, with Michelangelo-chiseled musculature, said Lynne Luciano, author of *Looking Good: Male Body Image in America.* Luciano is assistant professor of history at University of California, Dominguez Hills.

Lean and muscular physiques also are glorified in sports, TV, movies, music videos, advertising. They're even in toys. If GI Joe Extreme—the enhanced version—had been life-size, Luciano said, he would have a 32-

inch waist, 44-inch chest and impossible 32-inch biceps.

The danger of these images, Olivardia said, is they create a blueprint for the masculine man that is difficult for most men to follow without resorting to drastic, unhealthy measures, such as taking steroids, muscle-enhancing supplements, using laxatives, working out obsessively, becoming anorexic and/or bulimic.

Other factors

Distorted body images and eating disorders are often the manifestation of other problems, Olivardia said. Low self-esteem in childhood, adolescence and adulthood, psychological, emotional and mental issues can drive men to focus on their body or specific parts such as the midsection and see themselves as incredibly physically flawed.

Some people with a history of obsessive behaviors carry these over into their eating habits as a form of control, said Sarah Steinmeyer, psychologist at South Coast Medical Center Eating Disorders Program in Laguna Beach, California.

"Eating disorders are rarely about food," she said. "Food is a metaphor for other aspects of life. A man with an eating disorder and body obsession sometimes thinks he can control food, but food actually controls him."

South [Orange] County [California] resident Terry Murphy, 53, loathes what he sees when he looks in the mirror—an out-of-shape, overweight man. At 6 feet and 210 pounds, the management consultant said he feels he has no control over his body and is depressed about it.

"I can't get it out of my mind," Murphy said. "I think about it at least a dozen times a day."

Magazines . . . have perpetuated the myth that the look of male health is lean, low in fat, with Michelangelo-chiseled musculature.

Murphy, who said he never had weight issues before, put on pounds over the years when a heart condition prevented him from maintaining six-days-a-week, one-and-a-half-hour intense workouts. Murphy continues to exercise most days of the week, but has reduced the intensity for the sake of his heart.

So he diets. His breakfast: a regular-size beef patty and cottage cheese. Lunch consists of a protein drink and a banana or an apple. Dinner is a low-calorie salad with chicken, half a glass of milk and the occasional small cookie.

The secret shame

Dick, like Murphy, feels frustrated and alone.

"Ever since I can remember, my physical appearance has been a way of gauging my self-worth," Dick said.

Dick's weight for most of his teens was normal, but when he turned

19, he gained weight. At 5 feet, 6 inches, he weighed 195 pounds. After a routine physical exam, the doctor told him he was obese.

To lose weight, Dick did several things. He starved himself in private. And when he ate out with friends, he consumed a normal amount of food. But shortly after, he would excuse himself from the table, go to the public restroom and make himself vomit. "The sooner I could purge, the easier it would be to get the food out," he said.

He exercised relentlessly most days of the week, sometimes more than once a day.

Within a year, he lost 40 pounds.

Dick knew what he was doing was not healthy. But he kept it a secret. He was ashamed to talk about it with anyone. "It's a girl's disease," he said.

In 1989, a roommate caught him purging. At the friend's urging, he found a doctor who treated eating disorders. "The doctor tried to scare me with statistics and stories of girls who had died because of ruptures to their esophagus. I went three times for regular counseling. And then, I stopped. I thought I could do this on my own."

And he stopped bulimic behavior for six years. His weight stabilized at about 155 pounds. But his esophagus had been damaged from years of regurgitating food.

After a painful divorce several years ago, Dick returned to some unhealthy behaviors.

He takes nothing but coffee throughout the day. His only meal is at night.

"I don't know that I'm over it," he said.

A lack of groups

Dick has tried to look for local men's support groups—to no avail. He does not feel comfortable attending women's anorexia and bulimia support groups. "That happens fairly often to men who are trying to get help," Steinmeyer said. "And that's terrible because the lack of support groups for men only perpetuates the myth that this is only a woman's disease."

When men seek help, they are in the advanced stages of their eating disorders because it takes them a long time to recognize and admit that they have a serious health problem and to develop the courage to communicate their need for help, said Jane Supino, executive director for the Center for the Study of Anorexia and Bulimia in New York.

Treatments for men are the same as women's—they are tailored to the individual. They vary from outpatient visits to hospital confinement for days, weeks or months. They may include intense nutritional intervention, such as intravenous feeding, if needed. Olivardia said treatment programs that target the problems from many angles with a team approach—involving the primary doctor, a psychologist or psychiatrist, a nutritionist and support groups—are likely to have the best results.

5

Adolescence: Setting the Stage for Eating Disorders

Marlene Boskind-White and William C. White Jr.

Marlene Boskind-White, a professional counselor, has a private practice in Roanoke, Virginia. William C. White Jr., a clinical psychologist, was director of the Gannett Mental Health Clinic at Cornell University at the time of writing. The authors cofounded the Carriage House Clinic in Virginia, which they managed for many years.

Young girls and boys start learning to hate body fat very early in life. Even before the onset of adolescence, they already learn the message of "desirable slim bodies" from various sources: the home, the school, the mass media, and their peers. Girls, however, are more prone to dwell on the matter internally. Boys, in general, look out for activities to wrestle out their insecurities; girls, on the other hand, react passively by turning in toward themselves. As a result, girls are more prone to depression, which is one of the triggers for eating disorders.

In 1978 researchers at the University of Cincinnati College of Medicine examined the attitudes and preferences of preschool-age children in an effort to find the age at which antifat concepts emerge. Overwhelmingly, most (91 percent) preferred a thin rag doll over a fat one. The handful of overweight children in the study also chose the thin doll, although they could not say why. As early as three to five years old, then, there is a certain stigma attached to being overweight, and selective pressures on female children may have already been implanted. Other long-standing childhood studies support the findings that children develop a distinct aversion to chubby bodies and prefer athletic lean ones.

In 1967 Dr. J.R. Staffieri of the University of Indiana presented six- to ten-year-old male boys with silhouettes of obese, normal, and thin bodies. Uniformly, the subjects reacted unfavorably to the fatter ones. Furthermore, they attributed disparaging characteristics to the "fatty," labeling it as dirty, lazy, lying, sloppy, mean, ugly, and stupid. In 1972 Staffieri showed the same silhouettes to female children. They too reacted unfavorably to the fatty but added even more negative characteristics to their descriptions of it.

So it seems that both boys and girls disparage fat in childhood; however, beginning with adolescence, females overwhelmingly become more influenced than males. In 1971 Dr. E. Clifford at the Duke University Medical School found that 194 adolescent females aged eleven to nineteen were more dissatisfied with and critical of their bodies than 146 males of the same age range. A later study at the University of Iowa revealed that girls were beginning to undergo a distortion of body image, believing that they looked quite a bit heavier than they were. Eighty-six girls (ages ten to eighteen) from the Iowa City schools consistently overestimated the girth of their bodies. These studies indicated that young females wanted to be smaller but believed themselves incapable of attaining this ideal. Many experts in eating disorders believe these early childhood attitudes persist and may contribute to self-loathing and poor self-esteem in those who gain weight at later ages and could create extreme self-consciousness in anyone who fears becoming overweight.

It is not just the often quoted cliché of "the fear of growing up" that is the problem but the reality of growing up in a society that is clearly hostile, dangerous, and damaging to women.

The cultural message to be slim is transmitted to the child through many sources—the family, the child's peer group, teachers, books, magazines, and television. Children try to behave in a way that is consistent with the beliefs and behaviors of people in the groups to which they belong. When all groups agree, certain values are introduced without question. In our culture, the message is clear: Slimness is best.

At the same time, there is much to encourage excessive eating and weight gain. An abundance of fast food products exists, and we are bombarded with manipulative advertising from the food industry. Junk foods and fast foods are described as luscious and mouth-watering, with consumers challenged to binge: "Bet you can't eat just one!" Tempting snack foods help us to chew away our leisure hours. The presence of food is tied to recreational events and socializing, with cookouts, clambakes, and picnics part of the American way of life. We are led to snack during movies or while watching television. Children and teenagers are especially susceptible to this kind of advertising.

Hatred of fat and self

If both boys and girls disapprove of fat in childhood and yet experience simultaneous conflicting messages to be slim and to eat excessively, what happens in adolescence to escalate this hatred of fat and self in girls? The answer seems to lie in the socialization rituals to which both sexes, but particularly women, are exposed. What are these socialization rituals and how are they conveyed? What are the subtle as well as overt pressures that encourage smallness of mind and body in adolescent girls? . . .

For boys, signposts along the road to masculine identity have always been clear and well-defined. "To be a man" implies strength of character, courage, and the willingness to take risks and become independent. Until recent years, "to be a woman" meant serving and caring for other people. Men were taught to be outwardly directed and "to make a go of it" before settling down and taking on new responsibilities and obligations. Men have been conditioned to move away from their original families and to find primary fulfillment through work. Women, on the other hand, have been directed away from their families of birth to form new families in which caring for husbands and children has been expected to provide the ultimate fulfillment. . . .

Self-concept evolves through social interaction and is largely a product of socialization. There is now evidence that parents, especially fathers, regard their male and female infants in different ways based solely on the infant's gender. Although infant girls may weigh more at birth and actually be hardier than comparable boy infants, they are still viewed as weaker and more fragile.

When children enter nursery school, teachers often react differently to boys and girls. One study of nursery-school children reported that girls were encouraged to cling and ask many questions, while boys were taught to do and to be active. Other researchers report a sharp rise in "people orientedness" among girls at about the age of ten. Throughout adolescence, girls are more dependent than boys on the favorable opinions of others. Self-consciousness (as opposed to a sense of self) increases in girls and decreases in boys as they begin to mature.

Trained to seek approval

Success experiences in adolescence are, of course, crucial in developing a sense of confidence and self-esteem. However, researchers have found that girls begin to value *interpersonal success* more than boys at this time. Girls depend so much for their identities on relationships with others, especially boys, that rejection can be devastating. Boys certainly experience rejection in relationships, but they are in the process of forming identities that can sustain them. The young male is admonished to "act like a man" when disappointed and to "pick himself up" and carry on. By the time boys reach adolescence, they have had much more experience dealing with criticism, defeat, and rejection.

Witness any typical adolescent dance! The boys are lined up on one side of the dance floor, the girls on the other. The twelve-year-old boy ventures across the floor as his male friends watch carefully. When he reaches the chosen girl, he asks her to dance. She refuses. Amid the hoots and jeers of his peers, the young boy must traverse the endless distance back to his friends. He may feel little and small, but he does not *act* it. His socialization has already taught him that men do not allow themselves to be brought down by such experiences.

Girls, on the other hand, are reinforced for dependent and approval-seeking behavior. With little experience in developing confidence and autonomy, they carry a greater fear of rejection than do boys. This fear, when combined with an obsessive preoccupation with boys, can become a prominent and primary psychological characteristic of adolescent girls, leading to irrational and crippling fantasies about their own fragility, helplessness, and powerlessness! Confidence in being able to cope with their environment is thus eroded by such paralyzing fears and expectations related to the horrors of rejection. . . .

Mary Pipher (1994) believes that something dramatic is happening to adolescent girls in the 1990s and that they are having many more problems now than ten or twenty years ago! Preadolescent girls between seven and eleven are fairly well-adjusted and happy. Then something dramatic happens to them in early adolescence, causing their IQ scores to drop. They become less curious and more deferential and self-critical—especially about their bodies. They also become depressed. Pipher views the diluting of feminist values and the lip service paid to equality as a compelling factor. Add this to the growing *social problems* of more divorced families, chemical addictions, casual-sex, and the explosion of sexually transmitted diseases, as well as violence against women and soft- and hard-core pornography, and we are witnessing unprecedented stress on youngsters with a suicide rate among children aged ten to fourteen rising over 75 percent between 1979 and 1988. It is not "changing roles for women" that creates stress, misery, eating disorders, and other adolescent struggles. Girls are also subjected to increasing physical and sexual assaults, are more vulnerable, less secure, and more likely to have experienced upheaval and trauma in their lives, and are less free to strike out on their own in a landscape resembling a battlefield where date rape, herpes, AIDS, and drive-by shootings have become commonplace. Old stressors combine with new ones, creating suffering for all adolescent girls, not just those with eating disorders. It is not just the often quoted cliché of "the fear of growing up" that is the problem but the reality of growing up in a society that is clearly hostile, dangerous, and damaging to women. . . .

Passive response to stress

Many existing studies of depression in children support Pipher's clinical observations. Preadolescent children either evidence no gender differences in rates of depression or boys are somewhat more likely to be depressed than girls. Then sometime around the ages of thirteen to fourteen girls consistently begin to show higher rates of depression than boys, as much as two to one. The greater female rate of depression then continues throughout the lifespan for every adult age group except the elderly. . . .

Susan Nolen-Hoeksema (1995) identifies a feminine style of *coping* and proposes that throughout adolescence and adulthood women tend to have a more ruminative and passive style of responding to their own distress than men. This style of mood management exacerbates and prolongs periods of distress that arise for women and interfere with a woman's ability to overcome the negative events they face. . . .

[Rierdan has noted that] some of the biological and social challenges of adolescence that seem to enhance the development of eating disorders may be body dissatisfaction and pressure to conform to restrictive social roles deemed appropriate for females. . . . Many researchers have argued that both boys and girls who are dissatisfied with their bodies are more likely to become depressed. . . . Beginning in puberty, however, girls become more dissatisfied and thus more prone to depression. McCarthy (1990) suggests the more negative body image of girls leads many towards chronic dieting that *in itself* contributes to helplessness and depression.

In a series of studies of sixth, eighth, and tenth grade students, researchers found evidence that girls who accept a narrowing of activities and interests prescribed by the feminine gender role were at risk for higher levels of depressive symptoms. . . . Girls in sixth through tenth grades who spent more time in feminine-type activities—shopping, beauty rituals, and the like—exhibited higher depressive symptomology. On the other hand, those girls who resisted were rejected by peers. Showing one's competence and otherwise violating feminine stereotypes also led to depression. . . . Thus, these girls encounter consistent double-bind, or "catch-22," situations in which no matter what they do they cannot win.

The myth of feminine fragility must be banished, and young women must learn to identify positively with their bodies.

Researchers found that the more intelligent girls were, the more depressed they were. [A 1976 study by Rosen and Aneshensel notes that] girls increasingly want to conceal their intelligence as they go through adolescence. . . . This may explain the drop in IQ scores that Pipher has pointed out. More recent data find girls are still more concerned than boys about *others'* judgments of their appearance and behaviors. . . . Thus, it makes more sense to blame *femininity,* not feminism for these higher ratios of depression and eating disorders in girls.

One other important aspect of adolescence that must be mastered is the ability to form new and more mature relationships with one's own age group. Here again current research suggests that adolescent friendships among males reinforce movement toward activity and achievement while girls, fearful of being on their own, tend to cling to each other. While boys use friends as allies in efforts to break away from authority, girls often form intense conformist alliances, which researcher Janet Lever has referred to as "mini marriages." Much of their conversation centers around how to snare this boy or that one—in short, there is an excessive, often obsessional, amount of thinking about boys. . . .

Women should love their bodies

In our view, the general inability of adolescent girls to take pride in their bodies is one important reason why they have great difficulty establishing identities as women. Few realize that females are more durable physically than males. Consider that the female must be strong enough to nourish and carry the fetus through the prenatal period in order to insure the survival of the species. During the course of evolution, it is hypothesized that stronger females survived, while males, whose role in procreation does not require that kind of strength and endurance, were not selected for those qualities. The myth of feminine fragility must be banished, and young women must learn to identify positively with their bodies. This includes accepting and embracing changes that take place in the body. The bloating and weight gain that often accompany menstruation need not be viewed as unbearable. The pregnant female body, often associated with "unattractive changes" and the belief that "I will never have a perfect body again," should engender feelings of joy, power, and uniqueness, not self-loathing.

Emerging sexuality can also create enormous conflict in young women and increase the fear and distrust they have about their bodies. While they may be physically capable of the sexual act, few are ready for it emotionally. Our current mores present special problems. No longer is there the proscription to "save one's virginity." The so-called sexual revolution of the sixties did away with this important psychological protection. (To be fair, it was a proscription accepted by young men as well, at least as far as the "girls they were going to marry" were concerned.) Today the pressure to have early sexual experiences is intense and unrelenting. Understandably, many young women begin to think of themselves as victims. This feeling coincides with the time when they are beginning to receive special attention because of external attractiveness. All around, there are pressures that perpetuate the image of woman as ornamental, with her body the main commodity of worth. And behind this is the ultimate fantasy of attracting and capturing a man. Thus, "going along with him" and the "fear of losing him" can create overwhelming anxieties. The young girl is already learning to adapt to the desires and needs of others and, in effect, makes her own transformation into a sexual object.

Negative portrayal in advertisements

Advertisements further convince us that this is how women are or want to be. According to sociologists Gloria I. Joseph and Jill Lewis, advertising creates and shapes our values and fears so that we come to believe that imposed values/fears/attitudes/goals are our own, as if we had chosen them. In 1982 Joseph and Lewis conducted a survey of leading women's magazines to determine how female sex roles are presented and portrayed and to explore recurrent themes. They found that beauty ads comprised 68 percent of all advertising in *Cosmopolitan* magazine, and most women were portrayed as sexy, subordinate, and seductive, as competitors with other women, and as dependent on men. . . .

Television has become a major influence in the lives of children and also a major means of transmitting the values of society. Many social scientists are quick to point out that the recent wave of feminism has had an impact on television programming, and we can observe it, too. Women are now portrayed as doctors, lawyers, even truck drivers and display strength of character and courage. However, many commercials continue to portray women as insipid, mindless creatures, which may subtract from the influence of the new models of womanhood. Certainly, the commercials for sportswear carry a promise of all good things if the wearer is slim and a threat of failure if she is not.

Additionally, program material on television continues to reinforce a terror of being fat. Well-known actresses who over the years have appeared in movies and on television are significantly slimmer today. Some even appear too thin and unhealthy. One time, on several segments of *The Tonight Show*, almost without exception when women were conversing with each other, the focus was on dieting and the need to lose weight or on weight-related matters. One newly arrived South American singer remarked that she had left the poverty of her country for the United States "in order to eat." Now, after considerable struggle to get here, she had discovered that "she cannot eat!" . . .

Preoccupation with diet

Along with . . . antiobesity propaganda, there are extraordinary cultural persuasions to diet. We have come to believe that all life's problems can be solved by dropping pounds. Promises of success, transformation, an end to existential pain, and living happily ever after prevail. Myriad women (and some men) make a fetish of being thin and follow one reducing diet after another without knowing or caring that they can do so only at the price of severe anxiety and persistent health problems. Until very recently, being underweight was not considered as dangerous nutritionally as being overweight. Dr. Hilde Bruch believes that chronic malnutrition resulting from an abnormal preoccupation with weight is common but not readily recognized as abnormal because it appears under the guise of desirable slimness. Medical experts are only now beginning to call attention to the health hazards of indiscriminate or fad dieting. . . .

As we can see, overweight is still viewed as "the problem," without regard for the frame of mind or underlying issues that led to the overweight—*if there were any to begin with*!

The women we have worked with describe a variety of different pressures that led to their first decision to diet. A majority were overprotected and unprepared for the new demands posed by socializing with the opposite sex. Their families were self-contained units and the girls, as adolescents, felt isolated and socially insecure. Significantly, few were actually overweight at the time. One woman describes how she felt prior to her first diet: "I was a junior in high school, very desperate—longing for a boyfriend. I had a shallow social life—lived in a fantasy world—had faraway crushes that never materialized, but even so, always felt that I wouldn't be able to handle them if I did. Somehow I believed a loss of eight pounds would magically transform me into the princess."

Dieting provides a sense of meaning and purpose—a distraction from pain, loneliness, and insecurity.

The wish for magical personality transformation is often associated with expectations of weight loss. Shyness, feelings of inadequacy, confusion about men, and even ignorance will disappear as each pound is shed. The adolescent girl hopes that a new personality will be handed to her without any effort on her part. Sleeping Beauty will be awakened by a kiss!

Many women also say that a rejection (generally by a boy) in adolescence was the traumatic event that precipitated their first diet. More often than not, however, the adolescent girl *fantasizes* that she has been rejected because she is too fat. Most actually never heard this from the boys who had rejected them. For example, the two women whose words follow are certain that their fat resulted in rejection even though they had no real proof that this was the causal factor:

"My first real boyfriend dropped me without any explanation. All I felt then was rage at myself for being so fat and ugly, and I vowed never to be that way again."

And the other says, "I had a boyfriend who dropped me inexplicably, and I tied it to being fat."

Pressures can also emanate from family members. Mothers who are themselves obsessed with dieting may express horror when their daughters gain a few pounds: "My mother made me very conscious of my chubbiness after my last summer at overnight camp (age thirteen). I gained nine pounds and was made to feel ashamed and guilty."

Fathers too can set the wheels in motion. Although their total time spent with daughters may be less than in the mother-daughter relationship, their influence is powerful. Many times their standards of attractiveness for daughters are high, and a chance comment such as "you've put on a little weight" can create a humiliating sense of inadequacy in girls. As one young woman, who desperately wanted to please her father, put it: "Ever since I can remember, I wanted to be thin. Thin was in and fat people just weren't as attractive. I thought my thin cousin was somehow better because she was so slender, and I can remember standing behind her in grade school wishing my legs (which were normal) were as thin as hers. I was absolutely traumatized at age fourteen when my father told me I had a fat ass. Somehow I think I just always wanted to be Daddy's daughter and couldn't bear the thought of losing loving nicknames such as 'little face' or 'little bit.'"

Extreme self-criticism

The overwhelming desire to please others coupled with extreme self-criticism is the essence of the problem. Debbie and Becky were especially vulnerable to this type of criticism because they were athletes. A similar vulnerability is evident in young dancers. Dr. L.M. Vincent, author of *Competing with the Sylph: Dancers and the Pursuit of the Ideal Body Form,* is a physician (also a dancer) who has observed many impressionable young dancers forced by the weight obsessive dance subculture into destructive eating patterns. In his book, he describes his anger, frustration, and surprise at seeing a young slim dancer he delights in—"about the healthiest little girl I know"—reduced to tears and instilled with an intense desire to diet by the casual criticism of a dance coach: "Watch your weight."

Once dieting is initiated, the process and the end result become as important as the factors that led to the diet in the first place. Dieting provides a sense of meaning and purpose—a distraction from pain, loneliness, and insecurity. Many girls derive feelings of power from this form of self-denial. Others derive secondary gains for their vigilance. Friends are admiring and in awe of the self-denial required to lose weight. "Gee, you've lost a few pounds!" can create temporary feelings of self-esteem, but there are often negative consequences as well. In their dieting efforts many young women begin to harbor obsessive, selfish, and competitive feelings toward other women, gloating secretly when others are overweight. While they may want friendship, their preoccupation with body and their shyness keeps them from gaining friends (or from being a good friend themselves).

6
Bulimia May Be Linked to Sexual Abuse

Jennifer Redford

Jennifer Redford is a physician assistant in the Department of Obstetrics and Gynecology at New York Hospital in Queens.

Bulimia and other eating disorders are not the simple result of the misuse of food. They are complex diseases, manifested in the obsession with food and weight, but rooted in psychological malfunctions. Recent studies show that a history of sexual abuse is associated more with bulimia nervosa than with any other eating disorder. Experience of sexual abuse makes women vulnerable to such behavior as depression, anxiety, sleep disturbance, irregular sexual behavior, and eating disorders. Because symptoms are often common and vague, medical practitioners should inquire on eating habits, watch for danger signs of bingeing and purging, and carry out routine inquiries on mental health status and possible dysfunctional family environment.

The National Committee to Prevent Child Abuse defines sexual abuse as forced, tricked, or coerced sexual behavior between a young person and older person. In 1997, sexual abuse cases constituted 109,250 of 3,195,000 reported cases of child abuse. Young girls are 3 times more likely than young boys to be victims of sexual abuse, and 20 percent of American women report being abused as children.

Epidemiologic studies suggest that a history of sexual abuse predisposes some victims to the development of various psychopathologies such as depression, anxiety, sleep disturbances, aberrant sexual behavior, and eating disorders. In 1977, 7 million Americans, 99 percent of them women, reported suffering from eating disorders. The high prevalence of eating disorders among women who were sexually abused as children and the possibility that these phenomena may be related have gained the attention of social scientists. Further exploration of the data suggests that a history of sexual abuse may be more closely associated with bulimia nervosa than with other eating disorders.

Clinicians caring for women must be aware of and appreciate the complexity of this issue and understand why some sexually abused women can develop eating disorders in the absence of other psychiatric disorders. This article examines whether a relationship between childhood sexual abuse and the development of eating disorders exists and discusses the implications for health care providers and the management of eating disorders.

Bulimia serves as a ritual of "self-purification," providing a sense of goodness as the victim unconsciously experiences guilt and shame over the role her physical appearance played in perpetuating the abuse.

Despite the misleading nomenclature, eating disorders do not result from the simple misuse of food. Rather, anorexia nervosa, bulimia nervosa, and binge eating disorder are complex diseases with a common theme of food/weight obsession used to mask underlying psychopathologies. These disorders represent a maladaptive coping mechanism employed to deal with underlying difficulties with relationships, trust, unresolved childhood conflicts, and issues of self-worth. The theory that childhood sexual abuse frequently leads to pathologic behaviors such as eating disorders is plausible.

Some authorities propose that the nature of the abuse may influence the particular type of eating disorder that evolves. Because studies have found a greater incidence of bulimia nervosa among eating disorder patients who have been sexually abused, researchers hypothesize that more of these victims develop bulimia than other eating disorders. Experts speculate that personality traits and familial characteristics play a more significant role in the development of anorexia and binge eating disorder than does sexual abuse.

Connecting sexual abuse and bulimia nervosa

Ascertaining the exact impact of sexual victimization on mental illness is difficult because many other risk factors contribute to pathologic behavior. Beckman and Burns studied 540 college women and found that 49 percent of bulimic women reported a forced sexual experience compared with 27 percent of nonbulimic women. In a randomized telephone study of 3006 American women, Danksy and co-authors found that a greater proportion of bulimic women versus control subjects had been raped before age 11. Among a cohort of 4285 women, Garfinkel and coworkers found childhood sexual abuse to be 3 times more common among bulimics than among nonbulimic control subjects. An investigation of 72 bulimic women identified by the Bulimic Investigatory Test, Edinburgh (BITE), found significantly higher rates of sexual abuse committed by an adult relative for these women than for a nonbulimic control group.

Eating disorder specialists have proposed that the acts of purging and other compensatory behavior exhibited by bulimic women (e.g., vomiting, laxative and diuretic abuse, excessive exercise) are the key aspects correlating bulimia nervosa with a sexually abusive past. In 1 study, 75 percent of patients with eating disorders who had been sexually abused engaged in compensatory and purging behaviors. One researcher found that women who used 2 methods of compensation (e.g., purging and laxative abuse) were twice as likely to have a history of sexual abuse than women who engaged in only 1 method.

An understanding of the long-term sequelae of sexual victimization may help explain why bulimic behavior develops. Bingeing and purging behavior may be used as a distorted response to and a survival strategy after the abusive event. Clinical psychologist Rodney Demichael suggested that the sexually abused child "shuts off" the traumatic event from consciousness, which can result in partial or full amnesia. Although dissociation serves a protective function, it also prevents the individual from acquiring the coping skills needed to confront the abusive memories. Because normal adaptive skills fail to develop, the survivor can manifest eating disorder behaviors subsequently at developmental milestones, when she is called upon to confront new maturational issues.

Bulimic behavior is used to avoid intolerable internal states . . . caused by family stresses and memories of the sexual abuse.

Experts have similarly concluded that the binge-purge cycle is very symbolic. Abraham and Lewellyn-Jones suggest that symptoms develop as "highly effective ways to protect, repress, complete, divert, and numb memories of abuse." Kearney-Cooke believes that bulimia serves as a ritual of "self purification," providing a sense of goodness as the victim unconsciously experiences guilt and shame over the role her physical appearance played in perpetuating the abuse.

Bulimics may also use food as a readily available comfort tool that fills the void of empty interpersonal relationships the survivor has learned to distrust. Purging may also allow the bulimic to recover an illusory sense of control that is lost in an abusive relationship. Also, in attempting to make the body thin and unattractive, the individual may hope to ward off further sexual advances. The failure of bulimics to lose substantial amounts of weight, unlike anorexic patients, may perpetuate this cycle of self-destructive behaviors.

Although there appears to be a correlation between sexual victimization and bulimia, clinicians should not misinterpret the research and establish an overly simplistic "cause and effect" relationship between the 2 phenomena. Childhood sexual abuse cannot be considered the sole causative factor in the development of bulimia because other variables are known to play mediating roles. Kinzl notes that differentiating the effects of childhood sexual abuse from the effects of a dysfunctional family background may be difficult. In fact, parental psychological maltreatment as well as poor familial interactions may be just as operant in the etiology of bulimia. Therefore, it is beneficial to acknowledge a multidimensional etiology in the development of this complex disease. . . .

Perhaps a universal definition of sexual abuse may provide consistency among studies and allow more accurate data collection. Because there is conflicting data regarding the link between sexual abuse and bulimia, further exploration of the relationship is warranted.

Anxiety, depression, and withdrawal

The development of post-traumatic stress disorder (PTSD) may help explain the apparent relationship between sexual abuse and the subsequent development of bulimia nervosa. This syndrome can surface months to years after persons witness or are involved in an extremely traumatic event. Whether they have witnessed a natural disaster or have been victimized by sexual abuse, they can experience a common physiologic arousal and symptomatology as they continuously relive the event.

In PTSD, increased cortisol and catecholamine output is observed when intrusive memories or flashbacks are recalled. Symptoms of PTSD related to chronic sympathetic and adrenocortical activation include "anxiety, depression, impaired social functioning and withdrawal, general physical discomfort, as well as a higher incidence of premenstrual symptoms."

Because reactivity varies among individuals, not everyone involved in a traumatic event will develop PTSD; however, a traumatic event does render the person more susceptible. For example, PTSD appears to be more common among sexually abused bulimics than among persons with other eating disorders. Dansky's research found that 1 in 5 respondents with bulimia currently had PTSD and 1 in 3 had suffered from PTSD in their lifetime, with a 36.9 percent lifetime prevalence rate.

Experts are still investigating 2 possibilities: whether abuse survivors develop PTSD and an eating disorder independently or whether the eating disorder manifests as a direct response to the anxiety associated with PTSD. In either case, bulimia symptoms may represent instrumental coping efforts to manage the noradrenergic, serotonergic, and dopaminergic fluctuations that accompany memories of abusive events. Bingeing and purging are used as an "escape from the painful subjective experience associated with such pervasive neurotransmitter dysregulation."

Heatherton and Baumeister have similarly concluded that bulimic behavior is used to avoid intolerable internal states associated with PTSD caused by family stresses and memories of the sexual abuse. Furthermore, impulsive and self-destructive behaviors commonly observed among bulimics can be attributed to this heightened physiologic arousal. Therefore, the physiologic and psychological data observed in these investigations support the diagnosis of PTSD in women who have survived sexual abuse.

Implications for health care providers

Western countries are currently experiencing an epidemic of bulimia nervosa affecting all socioeconomic groups. Clinical epidemiologic evidence reports a 1 percent to 5 percent lifetime prevalence. However, questionnaire surveys reveal that up to 19 percent of female students confess to suffering from bulimia at some point. Due to the secretive nature of this illness, current clinical statistics represent only a minimum estimate of the actual prevalence within the community.

Primary care providers should become familiar with the clinical presentation and danger signs associated with bulimia because they are likely to encounter bulimic patients. Unlike the telltale body habitus of anorexics (emaciated body) and binge eaters (overweight body), bulimics have no pathognomonic body habitus. They can be underweight, normal weight, or slightly overweight. Indeed, the essential diagnostic criteria of bulimia is that sufferers often maintain normal weight. . . .

Health care professionals should be alert for red flags associated with bulimia: vague complaints of fatigue, lethargy, bloating, nausea, constipation, and abdominal pain. Calluses on the dorsum of the hand, resulting from induced vomiting, and electrolyte disturbances (e.g., vomiting-induced hypokalemia, hypomagnesemia, hyperamylasemia, hypochloremic alkalosis) are reliable signs. A morbid preoccupation with food and weight may also be evident.

Because eating disorders are common and symptoms are so vague, practitioners are advised to routinely question every young female patient about weight control and bingeing and purging behaviors, even when no obvious symptoms are present. Unless directly asked, patients are unlikely to volunteer the presence of pathologic behavior. Simple inquiries about usual meal and eating habits may serve as neutral openers. Unrealistic emotions about weight or body image should signal the practitioner to continue questioning to determine if an eating disturbance exists. . . .

Sexually abused bulimic subjects report previous suicide attempts . . . [and] have a higher incidence of . . . drug and alcohol abuse, shoplifting, sexual promiscuity, and self-mutilation.

The practitioner should also gather information about past psychological health. Routine inquiries on mental status, dysfunctional family environment, and history of sexual abuse are warranted in any examination. Therapist Kearney-Cooke suggests that clinicians preface this inquiry with a reassuring statement that many clients with eating disorders had unpleasant or distressing childhoods or sexual experiences and then ask whether anything of this nature happened to the patient. Clinicians should be able to listen to these accounts without becoming overwhelmed.

Thus, the health care provider can ascertain if past sexual abuse is affecting present mental health. This becomes especially important when dealing with sexually abused bulimics who may have a more serious clinical presentation. Psychiatric comorbidity, including depression, borderline personality or anxiety disorders, and chemical dependency may further contribute to the complexity of the clinical picture.

Fullerton and colleagues also observed that 52 percent of sexually abused bulimic subjects report previous suicide attempts. In addition, they tend to have a higher incidence of impulsive behaviors such as drug and alcohol abuse, shoplifting, sexual promiscuity, and self-mutilation. A history of sexual abuse may interfere with successful treatment of these severe symptoms. Failure to recognize these underlying factors may jeopardize treatment outcomes.

Treatment and outcomes

A comprehensive treatment plan is necessary to successfully manage bulimia and associated comorbidity. Effective treatment of bulimia may require both pharmacologic and psychotherapeutic interventions (e.g., cognitive-behavioral, group, and family therapies). Tricyclic antidepressants, monoamine oxidase inhibitors, and atypical antidepressants, such as fluoxetine, may be successful in lessening the severity of binge-purge episodes. Studies have reported that 50 percent to 90 percent of bulimics binge less when treated with antidepressants.

Although medication can break the initial binge-purge cycle, it is not sufficient alone to cure the disorder. Failure to recognize and confront any underlying issue, including sexual abuse, is cited as a reason for frequent relapse in the recovery of bulimia. Therefore, traditional treatment protocols must be tailored. Successful treatment should address substance abuse, psychiatric comorbidity, PTSD symptoms, and self-destructive behavior.

Frequently, the goal of treatment is to overcome long-term patterns of self-revictimization and help develop appropriate coping strategies. Primary care clinicians must be willing to refer patients to specialists trained to manage eating disorders. Once the patient is referred, the primary provider should continue to communicate with her. This maintains continuity in the provider-patient relationship and allows the provider to monitor any progress or relapses that may occur.

Even with comprehensive treatment, outcomes are variable. According to Hsu, 50 percent of bulimics remain asymptomatic for 2 to 20 years after diagnosis, 50 percent sustain bulimic behavior with episodic remissions, and 20 percent remain symptomatic.

A larger number of bulimic women report a history of sexual abuse than those with anorexia and binge eating disorder. Although no simple, direct cause-and-effect relationship exists, some experts believe that bingeing and purging behavior may represent a distorted response to and survival strategy after the abusive event. However, not all authorities believe that a likely causal relationship between bulimia and sexual abuse exists at all.

Clinicians caring for female patients should maintain a high index of suspicion for bulimia. The management of bulimia involves a multidisciplinary approach that includes antidepressants and psychotherapeutic interventions.

7

Bingeing and Dieting as Methods of Coping with Pain

Becky W. Thompson

Becky W. Thompson is the author of the book A Hunger So Wide and So Deep: American Women Speak Out on Eating Problems. *She was visiting assistant professor of African American studies and sociology at Wesleyan University at the time of writing.*

This essay, based on interviews with African American, Hispanic, and lesbian women, rejects the notion that eating disorders are only signs of women's vanity and obsession with thinness. The eighteen women—who took part in the author's life history project—often took refuge in food to escape from the ravages of poverty, racism, dislocation, sexism, sexual abuse, and other forms of traumatic experiences. This challenges the belief that eating problems occur only among white, well-to-do, heterosexual women. The article also notes that as a coping mechanism, an eating disorder does not really liberate women from their pain.

The connection between trauma and eating problems raises a key question: Why food? Why do women turn to food rather than some other way of coping? A common thread running through the stories of the women I interviewed is the power of food to buffer pain. Women across race, class, and sexuality began to diet or to binge to help them numb difficult emotions—rage, anger, loneliness, anxiety, fear. Like liquor, bingeing sedates, lessens anxiety, and induces sleep. Describing the effects of bingeing, the women said it "put me back to sleep after a nightmare," "made me numb out," "helped me stuff back emotions." Eating "was a break from the stress," a way to "deny all my feelings." Bingeing gave them a high, a feeling of contentment that countered the crying spells, nightmares, and depression that plagued many of them as children and young adults. Bingeing cut them off from uncomfortable and upsetting emotions.

The fact that many of the women first began to remember trauma-related dreams after they stopped bingeing suggests that eating large quantities of food, like abusing alcohol, can reduce one's dream state. (Alcohol abuse interrupts dream patterns, reducing the amount of rapid eye movement sleep.)

Although bingeing was the most common way these women numbed emotions, paradoxically, dieting served a similar function, helping them avoid painful feelings by giving them a goal—not eating—to focus on. This concentration, like the focus runners need before a race, distracted them from pain, anger, and confusion. Many initially binged, then learned to use dieting in a similar way as they grew older. They were ostracized or punished for bingeing, were told that an ample appetite is not socially acceptable for females, and were erroneously led to believe that weight gain is a direct function of eating. Had they been taught that a person's weight is influenced by a number of factors—including genetics, types of food eaten, and metabolism—not simply governed by self-control and counting calories, they might have been able to avoid the cycles of weight gain and loss associated with dieting. Instead, they began to diet as a means of focusing their attention on something they could control—a socially acceptable focus beyond their pain.

Eating that began as a simple solution to pain then became a generalized response to stress.

The anesthetic power of bingeing and dieting makes sense, but why did the women choose food rather than alcohol or other drugs? One reason is that food is available to young girls who don't have the money or mobility to get other drugs. They were searching for a narcotic long before they had access to liquor, prescription drugs, or street drugs: the ages of these women when they were sexually abused ranged from four to twelve; the average age was seven. Other forms of trauma also hit early.

A few of the women's earliest memories were of their fathers beating their mothers. Several were victimized emotionally before they were five. Food was the most accessible and socially acceptable drug available. When they began to binge as young girls, they could simply go to the kitchen for food. Those who did not have direct access to food stole money from their mothers' purses, took their classmates' lunches, and hid food for when they needed it. The availability, accessibility, and affordability of food made it their drug of choice.

Reaction to stress

Eating that began as a simple solution to pain then became a generalized response to stress. While a few of the women began to use other drugs as they grew older, most continued to turn to food. Trepidation about alcohol and illegal drugs kept some focused on food. Those who grew up with an alcoholic parent—or two—learned early the dangers of excessive drinking. Food seemed significantly less dangerous than alcohol, for them and for their children. Bingeing can also be less expensive than drinking.

Using food rather than drugs is partly a function of gender socialization and women's many responsibilities: you can binge at night and still get up in the morning, get children ready for school, and be clear-headed for college classes and work—without the hangover alcohol would cause. Women can overindulge in food and still do the work most women do: caring for children, driving, cooking, and holding down a job. When one woman's compulsive eating was at its height, she ate breakfast at home, stopped for a snack on her way to work, went to three different cafeterias for lunch, and snacked at her desk throughout the afternoon. Even when her eating had become constant, she was able to hold a job; eating enabled her to go on without falling apart emotionally. While that much food no doubt affected her productivity, being drunk or hung over would have been far worse.

Women raised in families and communities in which food was a sign of celebration naturally turned to food for comfort, but the pressures of assimilation and class expectations eventually denied them this consolation, and many went from bingeing to dieting. Many of the women who initially responded to trauma by purging and dieting were bombarded in childhood with messages that they should diet and be thin. For some, adolescence brought lessons in how to refine dieting techniques; a few were taught by family members how to be bulimic.

Bingeing and dieting are simple coping mechanisms because they are solitary. As children, many of the women were forced to rely on themselves as they reckoned with the loneliness that comes from a betrayal of trust. Children who are abused by family members have a vested interest in keeping the abuse secret; they often know the abuse is wrong but they are also aware that their families are "all" they have. Periodic fantasies of trading in their families for new ones are just that—fantasies. They know that reporting abuse could divide the family in possibly irreparable ways and leave them with no family at all. Many girls are programmed by abusers to believe the abuse is their own fault. Almost all of the women I talked with experienced trauma alone and, in many instances, had no choice but to endure isolation; they used methods of coping that maintained their anonymity.

With the knowledge that they could figure out ways to care for themselves, they regained power. A girl might not be able to stop her father from beating her mother, or make the children at school pay attention to her, or return to her native country, or make the welfare department provide decent assistance for women with children, but she *could* treat herself to food late at night, try to lose weight, or throw up food she wished she hadn't eaten. They knew not to tell others about their eating, and they could find ways to do it without getting caught. Those who dieted not only got a sense of control but also were praised for their discipline and willpower.

Coping with loss

Some of the women began to eat or to diet to cope with simultaneous physical, psychic, and spiritual losses. Some lost their belief in "god" and in the protection of a benevolent force. Those who were sexually abused lost trust in their caretakers; their bedrooms, homes, and playgrounds no longer felt safe. They also lost a sense of innocence, authenticity, and subjectivity and what Ellen Bass refers to as "the gift of anger." The girls whose mothers were beaten realized that their mothers' ability to protect and support them was limited. The battered mothers' confidence and hopes for the future were slight, and their daughters often lost a sense of possibility for themselves as well. Like the victims of sexual abuse, they too lost the sense of home as a safe place. Running away from home for extended periods of time—as three of the women did—was a telling indicator of being robbed of a refuge.

Some of the women began to eat or to diet to cope with simultaneous physical, psychic and spiritual losses.

For those who recognized their lesbian identities when they were young, acknowledging their sexuality meant losing family and friends. Those who came out were beaten by their parents, forbidden to see their lovers, told by their parents that they would rather have a *puta* (whore) than a *pata* (dyke) for a daughter, and persecuted at college by administrators and fellow students. The threatened loss of support was especially frightening to lesbians of color, since their families were their central link to their racial and cultural communities; they risked losing family and community simultaneously.

Moving to the United States ushered in enormous loss as immigrant women were cut off from the friendships, communities, families, rituals, smells, food, and music that they had grown up with. Adjusting to what are often perceived as the cold and distant ways of the United States left them feeling desperately alone, grieving for the comforts of home. While some gained more freedom of movement in the United States, the expectation that they would remain devoted and dedicated to their parents denied them independence and autonomy.

Poverty robs women of confidence and freedom. Poor women often have no car, which restricts their mobility. They can't enroll their children in a soccer league or buy themselves a new shirt without having to scrimp on food. Both small and big financial decisions are difficult when there is no money. And welfare subjects women to bureaucracy and humiliation while robbing them of independence and control.

Some of the women were able to grieve losses and disempowerment when they happened, but for others the grieving was postponed, leaving them overwhelmed and burdened by unfinished business. Financial or emotional demands robbed some of the women of the time and energy they needed to heal. Prolonged drug abuse and the numbed state that accompanies bingeing slowed the grieving process for others. Many of them experienced one trauma right on top of another, giving them little chance to make sense of events or to recover from them. . . .

In times of grief and sadness, food is an immediate companion. When as girls the women began to look for food in the middle of the night, they were searching for something they could count on to keep them company and help them get back to sleep. Metaphorically, their attempts can also be seen as a search for lost innocence. Some hunted all over their houses for sweets their mothers had hidden, searching for love and affection as well as for food. They wrestled with anger, confusion, and betrayal as pain rained down on them with such intensity that bingeing or dieting seemed their only comfort.

Food became a drug of choice for some as a consequence of the amnesia that characteristically follows many types of trauma, both physical and psychic. Most of the survivors of sexual abuse "forgot" the abuse and have only recently begun to retrieve memories of it. Those who endured the pain of heterosexist exclusion sometimes did not remember the details until adulthood. Those who were physically abused or saw others being hurt often did not begin to regain memories until many years later. These gaps in memory left them unable to explain or understand their feelings of shame, fear, depression, and loss. When the feelings or fragments of the memories resurfaced in dreams or when something reminded them of previous events, they could not attach their distress to its cause. This left them feeling out of control and confused. Some recall waking up with nightmares and searching for food; at the time they had no idea what caused the dreams or made them want to eat. Those who described feeling disconnected from the world or out of place at school had little idea at the time why they binged after school each day or purged in order to be able to binge without gaining weight.

Exclusion and discrimination

Individual amnesia is fueled by what [the poet] Adrienne Rich calls "historical amnesia," an erasure, glossing over, or distortion of history that occurs when an official version of history—which reflects those in power—is substituted for the actual stories of people's struggles against inequality. Two of the most obvious examples of historical amnesia are romanticized versions of Columbus's arrival in the Caribbean and nostalgic stories of the "taming of the West"—that is, the genocide of Native American people. . . .

> *While use of illicit drugs is typically associated with trying to create a new reality, bingeing and dieting, at least initially, allow a person to cope with an unavoidable reality.*

There are myriad repercussions of historical amnesia on individual lives. Among the women I spoke with, the young lesbians knew they were lonely and wished for more friends without knowing how to put a name to the source of their alienation. Historical amnesia has erased the history of lesbians who, despite isolation and loneliness, have survived and even thrived. As a consequence, they didn't understand the politics of their emotions; they did not have the language, memories, or political consciousness to understand what was causing their isolation.

The Latina and African-American girls who attended predominantly white schools knew they felt left out, but it was hard for them to articulate the social injustice behind their pain or to realize that they were not alone, crazy, or too sensitive. Instead, they were left to struggle alone against the historical amnesia evident in the myth that desegregation solved the problems of exclusion and discrimination in education. Situating individual struggle in a larger social reality is even more difficult for those who do not learn survival strategies from their families. Bingeing, dieting, and purging become understandable ways of numbing out amid this confusion.

Although the ability of bingeing and dieting to buffer pain explains how eating problems begin for girls across race, class, sexuality, and religion, the analogy between eating problems and drug use can only be taken so far. While food works like drugs by affecting mood, the dynamics are decidedly different. While use of illicit drugs is typically associated with trying to create a new reality, bingeing and dieting, at least initially, allow a person to cope with an unavoidable reality. Ultimately, this is why eating problems backfire: the ability to continue on can mask tremendous pain over many years. While bingeing, purging, and dieting may have saved them from abusive drinking, this is a mixed blessing because few people detected their problems, limiting the possibility of positive intervention. . . .

The progression of eating problems

Bingeing and dieting often begin as a sensible response to trauma, but eventually they usually cause problems of their own. Joselyn appropriately characterized them as "coping skills/antiskills," an accurate summation of how many of the women I interviewed described the progression of their eating problems.

Bingeing became a problem partly because, as they grew up, they increasingly internalized the cultural demand for thinness. Those who began to binge when they were only four or five years old were not self-conscious about their eating, nor did they necessarily feel guilty about it. They simply did it. Some were not yet aware of the popular misconception that all people who are fat "got that way" by eating too much, and therefore didn't know they would be blamed if they were big. By the time they were eight or nine years old, however, many had effectively internalized cultural messages about eating and their bodies: that their eating habits were the sole reason for their body size, that bingeing is a sign of lack of willpower and self-discipline, and that they should feel ashamed of having big appetites.

For many, dieting that began as a response to an invasion of their bodily integrity eventually hindered them rather than helped them control what they ate; cycles of bingeing and dieting undermined their confidence that they could control their eating. As a consequence of long-term dieting—which lowers metabolism—some of them found that they could only eat small amounts without gaining weight. Bingeing was a frequent reaction to hunger caused by dieting.

Had they not internalized the cultural ideology, their use of food to cope with childhood trauma might have remained simply that, but once they were familiar with bingeing or dieting, they continued to use these methods when they were faced with later traumas: rape, violent relationships, racist and heterosexist discrimination. Consequently, in addition to the physiological effects of cycles of dieting and bingeing, the women had to deal with the psychological effects of their method of coping. Bingeing, purging, and dieting helped them get by but did little to help them combat the source of their pain or to untangle the reasons behind their actions. In fact, bingeing and dieting often put on hold the emotional work they needed to do. . . .

Almost an addiction

Nicole describes her eating problems in three increasingly severe stages. In stage one, during her childhood, bingeing was neither conscious nor deliberate. She binged on whatever food was available and felt neither guilt nor remorse. During stage two, which began in college, bingeing became much more deliberate; for the first time, she began to steal food and to buy it in bulk. She attempted many diets and went on bingeing sprees with her best friend, who taught her to be bulimic. She was bingeing and purging for the same reasons she had binged in childhood—racist exclusion at school and her mother's physical and emotional abuse—but it had begun to be debilitating. Stage three began after college. She binged "no holds barred" and gained a lot of weight, topping three hundred pounds. . . . By stage three, the control over bingeing and purging she had when she was younger was gone as the physiological addiction to purging began to take hold. At this point, Nicole was in extreme physical danger since she could not stop herself from throwing up. What had begun as a protective response had turned on her, leading her to reach out for help.

The trajectory of most of the women's eating difficulties, however, was not as overtly progressive, which suggests that the framework of eating problems as an addictive disease cannot be applied universally. Many women binged, purged, or dieted during stressful or traumatic times: when the stress diminished, their problems with food subsided too; increased stress would cause their eating problems to flare up again. But—unlike those of the women whose eating problems were progressive and addictive—these eating patterns were no more intense than they had been during previous times in the women's lives.

> *Some methods of coping may serve women in the short term but may be counterproductive psychically or physically over the long term.*

In general, intermittent eating problems tended to be less physically and psychologically harmful than those described as progressive addictions. Among the women who characterized eating problems as progressive, most had been through several traumas when they were very young children. In addition, they appeared to have fewer means of escaping their pain than those whose eating problems flared up and subsided in response to specific stresses. For example, three women whose eating problems were progressive and addictive were African-American women who endured various types of abuse at home and experienced racist exclusion at school. Facing trauma both privately and publicly, they had nowhere to escape pain.

Life-threatening

Those who described not being able to leave their bodies as children were among those whose eating problems became progressively worse, to the point of becoming life-threatening. This suggests that leaving their bodies in the face of trauma may have protected some of the women from long-term consequences in a way not afforded to those who did not or could not escape psychically or physically. Whether the women's eating problems were progressive or intermittent, what began as helpful methods of coping eventually became impediments they decided to change.

The progression of eating problems over time illuminates why a strategy of resistance against a hostile and injurious environment is not necessarily the same as a strategy for liberation. In their research on African-American adolescent girls, Tracy Robinson and Janie Victoria Ward explain that while

> African-American people, particularly women, have become expert developers and appropriators of resistant attitudes, we believe that all these forms of resistance are not always in our best interest.

Some methods of coping may serve women in the short term but may be counterproductive psychically or physically over the long term. The progression of eating problems is a powerful example of how and why eating is not a strategy of liberation. As Ann Kearney-Cooke explains, "mechanisms that allow for psychic survival as an abused child become impediments for effective coping as an adult."

With the right resources and sources of support, the women I talked to began to heal—to develop sane relationships to food and their bodies—and to make the transition from surviving to flourishing, from resistance toward liberation.

8

Bulimia Is on the Rise Among Nonwhite Populations

Kathryn J. Zerbe

Kathryn J. Zerbe, a psychoanalyst, was director of the Adult Outpatient Department of the Menninger Clinic in Topeka, Kansas, while serving as medical director of the Women's Program, and staff analyst at the same institution at the time of this writing. For five years she managed the Eating Disorder Unit at the clinic. She was also on the faculty of the Karl Menninger School of Psychiatry until 1997.

Bulimia has been found recently to be on the rise among nonwhite groups such as African Americans, Hispanics, and Asians—a development that debunks the notion that the eating disorder mainly afflicts Caucasian populations. Kathryn J. Zerbe suggests that services should reach out more strongly to these groups as their cases may be unreported. Citing studies on increasing bulimia incidence in other countries, Zerbe notes that sociocultural change such as immigration, Westernization, and acculturation make communities vulnerable to the disorder.

Women of color in Western society have a lower incidence of eating disorders. However, this trend appears to be reversing itself, as more Hispanic and African American women feel the impact of media stereotypes and move into the middle and higher socioeconomic brackets that reward slender physiques. Although scientific data support the low incidence of eating disorders among these women, clinicians see eating disorders in all socioeconomic groups, races, and ethnic backgrounds.

Because eating disorders have been reported much less among African Americans, Asian Americans, and American Indians, clinicians sometimes fail to diagnose them in the nonwhite population. This oversight reflects a cultural bias and unintended yet prevalent bigotry. In addition, when an eating disorder is formally diagnosed in a nonwhite patient, inadvertent treatment problems may arise. Despite the best intentions of all involved, unconscious tinges of prejudice can undermine treatment. To move the treatment forward, mistrust and discomfort on the part of both the treater and the patient must be openly addressed. Because any of us may be unaware of some of our own prejudices, we must continually scrutinize our attitudes. This self-examination is especially necessary when two people from significantly different backgrounds work together.

A woman of color

Rose O., a 31-year-old African American woman with two school-age children, was brought to the hospital by her mother, who was a teacher. Having felt the pressure to become thinner at her job, Rose, a moderately obese young woman, had turned to bulimia and consequently had had several brief inpatient treatments for various related conditions. At least three times every year for the past 10 years, Rose had been admitted to hospitals for dehydration, fainting, and other residual effects of electrolyte imbalance. She was initially so ashamed of her weight problem that she would do anything to control it. As she began using up to 40 laxatives and diuretics a day, Rose also became "addicted" to the syrup of ipecac she used to induce vomiting.

Rose's husband had been less than supportive of her problems. He physically abused her on numerous occasions and often derided her mothering skills. Fortunately, Rose had the support of an involved mother and several good friends. They had encouraged her to attend local support groups, such as Overeaters Anonymous, which she initially had attended quite conscientiously.

> *Nonwhites who are underserved may have a higher incidence of eating disorders than reported.*

But nothing seemed to help Rose overcome her eating difficulties, and eventually she added shoplifting to her repertoire of self-defeating behavior. She even admitted to stealing different diuretics, laxatives, and ipecac in a final effort to lose weight by purging. The mental health professionals who worked with Rose in several settings suspected that her difficulties had deeper roots than she could acknowledge but found they could not seem to help her elaborate on her problems.

The fifth of 11 children, Rose reported growing up in a very happy family. She was glad to have many brothers and sisters, and she categorically denied having been abused either physically or sexually. Like her teacher mother, her father was a devoted parent. This hard-working couple was able to provide emotional and financial support for all their children. After graduating from high school, Rose received a scholarship to a major Southern university. She moved away from home and completed a degree in political science.

Rose's ambition to become a patent attorney was waylaid by her eating disorder. Despite her high LSAT scores, her obesity and race may have contributed to her rejection from admission into professional school. This possibility enraged Rose; and although some treaters who worked with her suspected that her belief was unfounded, eventual investigation proved otherwise. Rose had been subjected to three types of bigotry that had gone unacknowledged: she was a woman, she was African American, and she was overweight. Despite her aptitude, Rose was prevented from engaging in her chosen career. At first the rejections clearly lowered her self-esteem; later she decided she would do anything, including forceful efforts to lower her weight, so that she could pursue her goals.

Rose revealed this history only over a long period and with great difficulty. She acknowledged forthrightly that she did not trust her white treaters. Brought up to be egalitarian and fair, she found herself turning away from her family values that eschewed demagoguery because of her own experiences in the workplace. Her only joy seemed to be her two children, for whom she would sacrifice anything. Their welfare had pushed her to initially involve herself in treatment, only to later reject it before completion so she could return home to care for them.

Fighting for control

Rose's difficulty with trusting anyone was so intense that she tended to turn treaters into persecutors. At one point she even refused to eat or to drink, requiring her treaters to become more forceful in their attempts to care for her. Her actions clearly conveyed her lack of trust and symbolized her primary need to make others restrain her and force her into changing despite her own ambivalence. Previously Rose had met rejection involving her highest career aspirations with passivity; now she actively rejected those who attempted to assist her. Indeed, the more anyone attempted to motivate her to accept treatment, the more resolutely she avoided it. She was determined this time to be the ultimate victor in the fight for control over her life.

Rose's resistance also included avoiding having to share how badly she felt about herself vis-à-vis her color, her body, and the early impediments to her career. One could easily understand how difficult it would be for her to trust anyone she equated with those who had betrayed her out of hatred and intolerance. As a result, members of the interdisciplinary treatment team working with Rose often questioned their own value judgments that might be based on cultural and racial differences that would impede treatment. As we attempted to place ourselves in Rose's unfavorable position, we could see why she distrusted us. Sadly, her Pyrrhic victory over treatment was won by her own long-standing struggles with self-worth and reluctance to accept help.

[Asian] subjects who developed eating disorders maintained traditional practices and views and were not necessarily as concerned with body shape as were Westerners.

When Rose decided to leave treatment, those who worked with her were notably perplexed and sad. Why must it be, we asked, that differences like color or religion keep people apart when humans have so many basic similarities? We reflected on an observation Freud had made in the early 20th century about the composition of groups: small differences, and not the large ones as we might suspect, are what keep people apart. Thus we tend to emphasize differences like race and ethnic background that may unwittingly impede deeper communication and understanding among people rather than underscoring the similitude of all humans. As psychoanalyst Harry Stack Sullivan put it, "We are all much more human simply than otherwise," thus reminding us of the basic alikeness of all people. Even the conflicts of the emotionally troubled are not dissimilar from the "normal.". . .

Underreporting in nonwhite populations

Our staff members learned that because eating disorders have principally been recognized in the white female population, issues of culture, race, and ethnicity may be overlooked. Still, a number of case reports have described the occurrence of anorexia nervosa and bulimia nervosa in women of other races. Because all case reports are subject to methodological difficulties, they may actually underestimate the prevalence of these disorders in the nonwhite population. Service availability and usage may also factor into what disorders get reported and to whom. In England, women of black African descent have been quite vocal in complaining that psychiatric and medical services are less available to them than to the general population. Consequently, nonwhites who are underserved may have a higher incidence of eating disorders than reported. They are not receiving the help they need. This inference has significant implications for the health delivery system that must develop ways to help minorities acquire necessary treatment.

Traditionally, epidemiologic surveys carry more weight than single case reports. However, because they usually involve questionnaires, their results may also underestimate difficulties. Most surveys are conducted in easily accessible student populations, so the findings do not necessarily apply to divergent cultural groups where data are more difficult to retrieve. Surveys are also less reliable than information gained from personal interviews. Despite these caveats, some important information is nonetheless available.

Eating disorders might appear in different cultures at various times because of enormous changes that society is undergoing.

In the United States, two surveys have examined the eating attitudes and behavior of African American women. Applying strict diagnostic criteria, one group of researchers found that African American women had fewer eating difficulties than their white counterparts. A second study corroborated these results. Three percent of African American women met DSM-III (American Psychiatric Association 1980) criteria for bulimia, which was significantly less than a comparable group of white students (13 percent). Interestingly, African American and white subjects binged with about the same degree of frequency, but African American women reported less self-induced vomiting, laxative abuse, and diuretic use. Although more work must be done to understand why eating disorders are currently uncommon among African American students, the available studies incontrovertibly show that the prevalence of eating disorders is higher for whites than for African Americans.

A fascinating study by Nasser compared the eating attitudes of female Arab students studying at the University of London and Cairo University. She found that 22 percent of the students in London had impaired eating attitudes, in contrast to only 12 percent of those based in Cairo. Diagnostic interviews revealed that 12 percent of the London group met full criteria for bulimia, whereas none of the Cairo group exhibited bulimic symptoms. Westernization was also apparent in how the groups dressed. The London group of Arab students dressed like Europeans, in contrast to the more traditionally attired Cairo group. Although far-reaching conclusions cannot be drawn from this study alone, it supports the general impression that Westernization may push individuals along a continuum from dieting behavior to full-blown eating disorders.

Cultural changes engender eating disorders

Westernization has also affected Japan, where eating disorders are now well recognized and clinically prevalent. In densely populated urban areas, anorexia nervosa is reported to have an incidence of 1 in 500. However, bulimia in Japan is less frequently reported in research studies. One distinct binge-eating syndrome called *kibarashi* has also been identified. As a result, Japanese psychiatrists have established eating disorder units in hospitals that are now quite busy; anorexia and bulimia are reportedly becoming more common than Japanese scientific literature has indicated to date.

Two case reports describing anorexia in Africa point to the social and psychological conflicts engendered by cultural changes as leading to anorexia. How cultural tensions may signal the development of eating disorders was suggested by studies performed by Mumford and Whitehouse and Lee, who studied British, Asian, and Hong Kong schoolgirls. These investigators found that the subjects who developed eating disorders maintained traditional practices and views and were not necessarily as concerned with body shape as were Westerners. Those individuals who had eating disorders held onto their traditional ways of living and knowing, despite the great social shifts apparent in their environment.

In a paper examining the influence of acculturation on young women, Bulik described two cases of eating disorders in Eastern European immigrants to the United States. One subject met DSM-III criteria for bulimia, and another met the criteria for anorexia nervosa. When facing pressure in adapting to a new culture, reorganization of traditional family goals and values may be crucial elements in the development of eating disorders in these women. Bulik has suggested that attempting to become a part of the new culture may encourage one to overidentify with certain aspects of it. In this case, overvaluation of slimness probably led to the eating disorders.

Studies of the Hispanic population in the United States have also been meager. Dolan's 1991 study suggests no difference in treatment outcome between Hispanic and white patients. . . . However, it is difficult to infer much from a single study or a small population. More cross-cultural studies will help us better understand how changing attitudes of beauty and female roles foster eating disorders. The entire area merits much more investigation because of the information it will reap and the methodological flaws in the studies we currently rely upon.

On the rise in other countries

Suffice it to say that there is mounting evidence that cases of anorexia nervosa and bulimia nervosa are on the rise outside the Western world. Case reports of these disorders among many races are beginning to appear. In a letter to the *British Journal of Psychiatry*, Gandhi and colleagues noted that anorexia does occur on the Indian subcontinent; 5 new cases out of 2,500 referrals were presented to their clinic over a period of 4 years. Although one hypothesis about these trends might be that thinness was becoming more laudable in certain societies than it had been, an equally attractive idea might center on eating disorders as a cultural change syndrome. That is, eating disorders might appear in different cultures at various times because of enormous changes that society is undergoing.

By pulling these cultural and psychodynamic perspectives together, we might gain a clearer view of the overall situation. As indicated, eating is such a basic human activity that it carries many psychological meanings. Even tiny disruptions can easily get a person's eating off track. One might tend to react to cultural turmoil at times of transition by "choosing" an activity that is ubiquitous and symbolic, but also related to socialization and physiological integrity.

In the 1990s, transcultural studies are demonstrating how some societies undergoing rapid economic and sociocultural change may become more prone to eating disorders. This idea is an adjunct to the commonly touted culture-bound syndrome hypothesis, which posits that an emphasis on thinness and the body beautiful explains the female preponderance of eating disorders. However, a look at the history of anorexia nervosa reveals that eating disorders are not a modern disease, nor do they present themselves in the same way in all populations. Consequently, we know that the disorder can surface in disparate societies at various transitional times with quite dissimilar political, biological, and psychological meanings ascribed to it.

9

Current Approaches to Treating Bulimia

Carolyn Costin

Carolyn Costin, a recovered anorexic, is the author of The Eating Disorder Sourcebook *and* Your Dieting Daughter. *She has directed several inpatient eating disorder programs.*

Those who suffer from bulimia and other eating disorders should be informed of available treatment approaches and practices and choose what is best for them. There are three approaches, which may be used by clinicians individually or in combination. The first seeks to understand and treat the cause or causes of the eating disorder. The second, the most widely used so far, involves replacing distorted thoughts and behaviors with more positive ones. The third considers disordered eating as an addiction and applies practices that have been found effective in treating drug and alcohol addiction.

Depending on how clinicians view the nature of eating disorders, they will most likely approach treatment from one or more of the following perspectives:
- Psychodynamic
- Cognitive behavioral
- Disease/addiction

It is important when choosing a therapist that patients and significant others understand that there are different theories and treatment approaches. Admittedly, patients may not know whether a certain theory or treatment approach is suitable for them, and they may need to rely on instinct when choosing a therapist. Many patients know when a certain approach is not appropriate for them. For example, I often have patients elect to go into individual treatment with me or choose my treatment program over others because they have previously tried and do not want a Twelve Step or addiction-based approach. Getting a referral from a trustworthy individual is one way to find an appropriate professional or treatment program.

Excerpted from *The Eating Disorder Sourcebook: A Comprehensive Guide to the Causes, Treatments, and Prevention of Eating Disorders,* 2nd edition, by Carolyn Costin (Los Angeles: Lowell House, 1999). Copyright © 1999 by Lowell House. Reprinted with permission.

Psychodynamic model

A psychodynamic view of behavior emphasizes internal conflicts, motives, and unconscious forces. Within the psychodynamic realm there are many theories on the development of psychological disorders in general and on the sources and origins of eating disorders in particular. Describing each psychodynamic theory and the resulting treatment approach, such as object relations or self-psychology, is beyond the scope of this article.

The common feature of all psychodynamic theories is the belief that without addressing and resolving the underlying cause for disordered behaviors, they may subside for a time but will all too often return. The early pioneering and still relevant work of Hilde Bruch on treating eating disorders made it clear that using behavior modification techniques to get people to gain weight may accomplish short-term improvement but not much in the long run. Like Bruch, therapists with a psychodynamic perspective believe that the essential treatment for full recovery from an eating disorder involves understanding and treating the cause, adaptive function, or purpose that the eating disorder serves. Please note that this does not necessarily mean "analysis," or going back in time to uncover past events, although some clinicians take this approach. . . .

In all of the psychodynamic theories, symptoms are seen as expressions of a struggling inner self that uses the disordered eating and weight control behaviors as a way of communicating or expressing underlying issues. The symptoms are viewed as useful for the patient, and attempts to directly try to take them away are avoided. In a strict psychodynamic approach, the premise is that, when the underlying issues are able to be expressed, worked through, and resolved, the disordered eating behaviors will no longer be necessary. . . .

In all of the psychodynamic theories, symptoms are seen as expressions of a struggling inner self that uses the disordered eating . . . as a way of communicating or expressing underlying issues.

Psychodynamic treatment usually consists of frequent psychotherapy sessions using interpretation and management of the transference relationship or, in other words, the patient's experience of the therapist and vice versa. Whatever the particular psychodynamic theory, the essential goal of this treatment approach is to help patients understand the connections between their pasts, their personalities, and their personal relationships and how all this relates to their eating disorders.

The problem with a solely psychodynamic approach to treating eating disorders is twofold. First, many times patients are in such a state of starvation, depression, or compulsivity that psychotherapy cannot effectively take place. Therefore, starvation, tendency toward suicide, compulsive bingeing and purging, or serious medical abnormalities may need to be addressed before psychodynamic work can be effective. Second, patients can spend years doing psychodynamic therapy gaining insight while still engaging in destructive symptomatic behaviors. To continue this kind of therapy for too long without symptom change seems unnecessary and unfair. Psychodynamic therapy can offer a lot to eating disordered individuals and may be an important factor in treatment, but a strict psychodynamic approach alone—with no discussion of the eating- and weight-related behaviors—has not been shown to be effective in achieving high rates of full recovery. At some point, dealing directly with the disordered behaviors is important. The most well-known and studied technique or treatment approach currently used to challenge, manage, and transform specific food and weight-related behaviors is known as cognitive behavioral therapy.

Cognitive behavioral model

The term *cognitive* refers to mental perception and awareness. Cognitive distortions in the thinking of eating disordered patients that influence behavior are well recognized. A disturbed or distorted body image, paranoia about food itself being fattening, and binges being blamed on the fact that one cookie has already destroyed a perfect day of dieting are common unrealistic assumptions and distortions. Cognitive distortions are held sacred by patients who rely on them as guidelines for behavior in order to gain a sense of safety, control, identity, and containment. Cognitive distortions have to be challenged in an educational and empathetic way in order to avoid unnecessary power struggles. Patients will need to know that their behaviors are ultimately their choice but that currently they are choosing to act on false, incorrect, or misleading information and faulty assumptions.

Cognitive behavioral therapy (CBT) was originally developed in the late 1970s by Aaron Beck as a technique for treating depression. The essence of cognitive behavioral therapy is that feelings and behaviors are created by cognitions (thoughts). One is reminded of Albert Ellis and his famous Rational Emotive Therapy (RET). The clinician's job is to help individuals learn to recognize cognitive distortions and either choose not to act on them or, better still, to replace them with more realistic and positive ways of thinking. Common cognitive distortions can be put into categories such as all-or-nothing thinking, overgeneralizing, assuming, magnifying or minimizing, magical thinking, and personalizing.

Those familiar with eating disorders will recognize the same or similar cognitive distortions repeatedly being expressed by eating disordered individuals seen in treatment. Disordered eating or weight-related behaviors such as obsessive weighing, use of laxatives, restricting all sugar, and binge eating after one forbidden food item passes the lips, all arise from a set of beliefs, attitudes, and assumptions about the meaning of eating and body weight. Regardless of theoretical orientation, most clinicians will eventually need to address and challenge their patients' distorted attitudes and beliefs in order to interrupt the behaviors that flow from them. If not addressed, the distortions and symptomatic behaviors are likely to persist or return. . . .

Cognitive distortions help people explain or justify their behavior to others. Stacey, a forty-five-year-old anorexic, would always complain, "If I eat more I feel bloated and miserable." Barbara, a binge eater, would restrict eating sweets only to end up bingeing on them later, justifying this by telling everyone, "I'm allergic to sugar." Both of these claims are more difficult to argue with than "I'm afraid to eat more food" or "I set myself up to binge because I don't allow myself to eat sugar." Patients will justify their continued starving or purging by minimizing negative lab test results, hair loss, and even poor bone density scans. Magical thinking allows patients to believe and try to convince others to believe that electrolyte problems, heart failure, and death are things that happen to other people who are worse off.

A prudent course of action . . . would be to utilize cognitive behavioral therapy at least as a part of an integrated multidimensional approach.

Treating patients with cognitive behavioral therapy is considered by many top professionals in the field of eating disorders to be the "gold standard" of treatment, especially for bulimia nervosa. At the April 1996 International Eating Disorder Conference, several researchers such as Christopher Fairburn and Tim Walsh presented findings reiterating that cognitive behavioral therapy combined with medication produces better results than psychodynamic therapy combined with medication, either of these modalities combined with a placebo, or medication alone. Even though these findings are promising, the researchers themselves concede that the results show only that in these studies, one approach works better than others tried, and not that we have found a form of treatment that will help most patients. For information on this approach, see *Overcoming Eating Disorders Client Handbook* and *Overcoming Eating Disorders Therapist's Guide* by W. Agras and R. Apple (1997). Many patients are not helped by the cognitive behavioral approach, and we are not sure which ones will be. More research needs to be done. A prudent course of action in treating eating disordered patients would be to utilize cognitive behavioral therapy at least as a part of an integrated multidimensional approach.

Disease/addiction model

The disease or addiction model of treatment for eating disorders, sometimes referred to as the abstinence model, was originally taken from the disease model of alcoholism. Alcoholism is considered an addiction, and alcoholics are considered powerless over alcohol because they have a disease that causes their bodies to react in an abnormal and addictive way to the consumption of alcohol. The Twelve Step program of Alcoholics Anonymous (AA) was designed to treat the disease of alcoholism based on this principle. When this model was applied to eating disorders, and Overeaters Anonymous (OA) was originated, the word *alcohol* was substituted with the word *food* in the Twelve Step OA literature and at Twelve Step OA meetings. The basic OA text explains, "The OA recovery program is identical with that of Alcoholics Anonymous. We use AA's twelve steps and twelve traditions, changing only the words *alcohol* and *alcoholic* to *food* and *compulsive overeater*. . . . In this model, food is often referred to as a drug over which those with eating disorders are powerless. The Twelve Step program of Overeaters Anonymous was originally designed to help people who felt out of control with their overconsumption of food: "The major objective of the program is to achieve abstinence, defined as freedom from compulsive overeating." The original treatment approach involved abstaining from certain foods considered binge foods or addictive foods, namely sugar and white flour, and following the Twelve Steps of OA. . . .

The addiction analogy and abstinence approach make some sense in relationship to its original application to compulsive overeating. It was reasoned that if addiction to alcohol causes binge drinking, then addiction to certain foods could cause binge eating; therefore, abstinence from those foods should be the goal. This analogy and supposition is debatable. To this day we have found no scientific proof of a person being addicted to a certain food, much less masses of people to the same food. Nor has there been any proof that an addiction or Twelve Step approach is successful in treating eating disorders. The analogy that followed—that compulsive overeating was fundamentally the same illness as bulimia nervosa and anorexia nervosa and thus all were addictions—made a leap based on faith, or hope, or desperation. In an effort to find a way to treat the growing number and severity of eating disorder cases, the OA approach began to be loosely applied to all forms of eating disorders. The use of the addiction model was readily adopted due to the lack of guidelines for treatment and the similarities that eating disorder symptoms seemed to have with other addictions. Twelve Step recovery programs sprung up everywhere as a model that could be immediately adapted for use with eating disorder "addictions." This was happening even though one of OA's own pamphlets, entitled, "Questions & Answers," tried to clarify that "OA publishes literature about its program and compulsive overeating, not about specific eating disorders such as bulimia and anorexia."

Carefully monitor patients under Twelve Step

The American Psychiatric Association (APA) recognized a problem with Twelve Step treatment for anorexia nervosa and bulimia nervosa in their treatment guidelines established in February 1993. In summary, the APA's position is that Twelve Step based programs are not recommended as the sole treatment approach for anorexia nervosa or the initial sole approach for bulimia nervosa. The guidelines suggest that for bulimia nervosa Twelve Step programs such as OA may be helpful as an adjunct to other treatment and for subsequent relapse prevention. In determining these guidelines the members of the APA expressed concerns that due to "the great variability of knowledge, attitudes, beliefs, and practices from chapter to chapter and from sponsor to sponsor regarding eating disorders and their medical and psychotherapeutic treatment and because of the great variability of patients' personality structures, clinical conditions, and susceptibility to potentially counter therapeutic practices, clinicians should carefully monitor patients' experiences with Twelve Step programs."

Some clinicians feel strongly that eating disorders are addictions; for example, according to Kay Sheppard, in her 1989 book, *Food Addiction, The Body Knows*, "the signs and symptoms of bulimia nervosa are the same as those of food addiction." Others acknowledge that although there is an attractiveness to this analogy, there are many potential problems in assuming that eating disorders are addictions. In the *International Journal of Eating Disorders,* Walter Vandereycken, M.D., a leading figure in the field of eating disorders from Belgium, wrote, "The interpretative 'translating' of bulimia into a known disorder supplies both the patient and therapist with a reassuring point of reference. . . . Although the use of a common language can be a basic factor as to further therapeutic cooperation, it may be at the same time a diagnostic trap by which some more essential, challenging, or threatening elements of the problem (and hence the related treatment) are avoided." What did Vandereycken mean by a "diagnostic trap"? What essential or challenging elements might be avoided?

If a Twelve Step approach is to be used . . . it must be used with caution and adapted to the uniqueness of eating disorders.

One of the criticisms of the addiction or disease model is the idea that people can never be recovered. Eating disorders are thought to be lifelong diseases that can be controlled into a state of remission by working through the Twelve Steps and maintaining abstinence on a daily basis. According to this viewpoint, eating disordered individuals can be "in recovery" or "recovering" but never "recovered." If the symptoms go away, the person is only in abstinence or remission but still has the disease. A "recovering" bulimic is supposed to continue referring to herself as a bulimic and continue attending Twelve Step meetings indefinitely with the goal of remaining abstinent from sugar, flour, or other binge or trigger foods or bingeing itself. Most readers will be reminded of the alcoholic in Alcoholics Anonymous (AA), who says, "Hi. I'm John and I am a recovering alcoholic," even though he may not have had a drink for ten years. Labeling eating disorders as addictions may not only be a diagnostic trap but also a self-fulfilling prophecy. . . .

To be used with caution

Furthermore, behavior abstinence, such as refraining from binge eating, is different from substance abstinence. When does eating become overeating and overeating become binge eating? Who decides? The line is fuzzy and unclear. One would not say to an alcoholic, "You can drink, but you must learn how to control it; in other words, you must not binge drink." Drug addicts and alcoholics don't have to learn how to control the consumption of drugs or alcohol. Abstinence from these substances can be a black-and-white issue and, in fact, is supposed to be. Addicts and alcoholics give up drugs and alcohol completely and forever. A person with an eating disorder has to deal with food every day. Full recovery for a person with an eating disorder is to be able to deal with food in a normal, healthy way.

As has been previously mentioned, bulimics and binge eaters could abstain from sugar, white flour, and other "binge foods," but, in most cases, these individuals will ultimately binge on any food. In fact, labeling a food as a "binge food" is another self-fulfilling prophecy, actually counterproductive to the cognitive behavioral approach of restructuring dichotomous (black-and-white) thinking that is so common in eating disordered patients.

I do believe that there is an addictive quality or component to eating disorders; however, I don't see that this means that a Twelve Step approach is appropriate. I see the addictive elements of eating disorders functioning differently, especially in the sense that eating disordered patients can become recovered.

Although I have concerns and criticisms of the traditional addiction approach, I recognize that the Twelve Step philosophy has a lot to offer, particularly now that there are specific groups for people with anorexia nervosa and bulimia nervosa (ABA). However, I strongly believe that if a Twelve Step approach is to be used with eating disordered patients, it must be used with caution and adapted to the uniqueness of eating disorders. . . .

In summary, based on my experience and my recovered patients themselves, I urge clinicians who use the Twelve Step approach with eating disordered patients to:

1. Adapt them for the uniqueness of eating disorders and of each individual.
2. Monitor patients' experiences closely.
3. Allow that every patient has the potential to become recovered.

The belief that one will not have a disease called an eating disorder for life but can be "recovered" is a very important issue. How a treating professional views the illness and the treatment will not only affect the nature of the treatment but also the actual outcome itself. . . .

Norman Cousins, who learned firsthand the power of belief in eliminating his own illness, concluded in his book *Anatomy of an Illness*, "Drugs are not always necessary. Belief in recovery always is." If patients believe they can be more powerful than food and can be recovered, they have a better chance of it. I believe all patients and clinicians will benefit if they begin and involve themselves in treatment with that end in mind. . . .

The three main philosophical approaches to the treatment of eating disorders do not have to be considered exclusively when deciding on a treatment approach. Some combination of these approaches seems to be the best. There are psychological, behavioral, addictive, and biochemical aspects in all cases of eating disorders, and therefore it seems logical that treatment be drawn from various disciplines or approaches even if one is emphasized more than the others. Individuals who treat eating disorders will have to decide on their own treatment approach based on the literature in the field and their own experience. The most important thing to keep in mind is that the treating professional must always make the treatment fit the patient rather than the other way around.

10

The Role of Parents in a Child's Recovery

Abigail H. Natenshon

Abigail H. Natenshon—psychotherapist, author, and speaker—is the author of When Your Child Has an Eating Disorder: A Step-by-Step Workbook for Parents and Other Caregivers. *Her website www. empoweredparents.com offers practical help in helping victims of eating disorders.*

Parents often witness the deteriorating condition of a child who has developed an eating disorder, but their lack of awareness of the gravity of the disease often prevents them from acting in time to remedy the illness. Parents can help their children most by gently confronting them, helping them seek the most effective professional help, and cooperating with professionals as a responsible member of the treatment team.

Ninety percent of eating disordered victims are adolescents living at home with parents and families. Symptoms of these disorders (along with their recovery) are an integral part of daily living, unfolding before parents' eyes virtually everywhere—at the dinner table, in bathrooms, bedrooms and kitchens, in conversation and in attitudes. Parents and families become victims in their own right by virtue of living alongside the eating disorder phenomenon. Even the most competent and adept parents find themselves feeling defeated, at a loss for what to think, how to behave and how to support their child in the throes of this mystifying disease. They do not know what they should do, if anything, in response. Believing that they are the cause of their child's disorder, they assume that by intervening they would only make a bad situation worse.

Parents fear that the very mention of food or weight could inspire an eating disorder in their healthy child, particularly in light of the statistic that 80 percent of children in grades three to six express dissatisfaction with their bodies, and that eating disorders have become the disease of choice for the expression of anxiety in youth today.

Obstacles

Impediments to parental involvement in their child's eating disorder recovery:

- Parents frequently do not understand what eating disorders are really about or what they indicate about their child.
- Bombarded by societal norms that reinforce food and fat phobias, and beleaguered by misconceptions and stereotypes about eating disorders, many parents assume that it is a normal and acceptable rite of passage for teenagers to be obsessed with weight and to restrict food. Under the influence of fickle and often conflicting diet fads and trends, many parents have virtually forgotten what healthy eating is. Fat-free eating is not healthy eating.
- Parents assume that eating disorders are incurable, that "once eating disordered, always eating disordered."
- Clinicians are typically adamant about parents staying out of their child's treatment and their food, cautioning that such discussions would lead to power struggles, alienation, and frustration. Assuming that parental involvement is intrusive and prying rather than supportive, they consider it to be a deterrent to the child's budding autonomy and separation from the family, a threat to the child's privacy and the confidentiality of the treatment process. In fact, a parent's involved concern in no way precludes his or her respect for the child's privacy or independence. Similarly, a therapist need not breach therapy confidences by educating a parent to assist their child's healing.
- Assuming that reticence, irritability, disrespect, and rudeness are "normal" teenage behaviors, many parents believe that by the time their child has reached early adolescence, their influence will have been usurped by peers, social norms, and the media. In actual fact, parents inadvertently encourage emotional disconnection by relinquishing their authority over their children at increasingly younger ages. Seven and eight year olds are sent away to overnight summer camps. Twelve-year-olds are given full access to credit cards. Cell phones are often the primary means for communicating with teens on the go and behind the wheel. Kids are sent to school in the morning without a sack lunch. In 50 percent of American homes, the traditional family dinner has gone by the wayside as more households are becoming cooking-free.
- In a position to absorb their child's erupting pain, many parents feel threatened by their child's hostility or resistance to their advances. Seeing the parent/child relationship as a fabric so fragile as to unravel with the first pull of a single thread, many parents have little tolerance for the candor, criticism, hostility or sensitivity that confronting a disordered child might engender. The very existence of the eating disorder bespeaks the individual's need to avoid having to face and resolve problems squarely. Living alongside an eating disorder, recovery can be divisive and unsettling for parents, whether or not they become involved in the process. Treatment signifies change, and change may represent a risk too great for the child to tolerate comfortably.

Understanding eating disorders
and the parent's role in recovery

Many parents fail to recognize that they are dealing with a disease, and a lethal one at that. Eating disordered behaviors are frightening and incomprehensible to parents particularly when these individuals fail to grasp that the essence of the eating disorder is not so much in food as it is in the underlying emotional issues driving eating dysfunction. Anorexia and bulimia affect the child's cognitive mind, body, emotions and relationships; they are disorders of coping and problem solving, of distortion and extremes, of choicelessness and fear, of mood and physical function. A window into the emotional life and soul of the child, they provide parents an invaluable opportunity to recognize and correct emotional disturbances, immaturity, and attitudes that could otherwise derail the child's effective development into adulthood. Eating disorders are a green light for parents to take charge and take action in a situation where the child is consummately, and hopefully temporarily, out of control. Parents need to learn how and when to intervene.

Proactive parents respond to their eating disordered child on three levels;
1. by confronting the child
2. by searching out the most effective professional help
3. by partnering with professionals and child against the disease, as a committed member of the treatment team

Researchers at the Maudsley Psychiatric Clinic in London found that anorexic children living at home who have been ill for less than three years responded more effectively to conjoint family treatment than they did to individual psychotherapy. Parents are their child's most potent teachers; the most successful life lessons are taught through role modeling both a healthy eating lifestyle and effective problem solving. When their children were infants, parents knew how to feed them; somewhere along the line, they lost faith in the wisdom of their instincts. Parental roles in facilitating recovery will be varied and fluid, dictated by the changing needs and capacities of the child patient and by the requirements of disease and recovery. The nature and quality of parental involvement will be determined by intention and interpersonal skills, sensitivity to the child's needs, and the receptiveness of child and therapist. By advocating for their child's health, parents enhance the well-being of the entire family.

Many parents fail to recognize that they are dealing with a disease, and a lethal one at that.

With age and increased maturity, the child's need for external (parental) monitoring diminishes in response to increased internal controls. In instances where emotional development is interrupted, however, as in the case of the eating disordered adolescent, or when the malnourished child has lost her capacity for self-regulation through distortions and compulsion, she turns to the eating disorder to provide the control she lacks. Under these circumstances, it is the parents' right, obligation, and in fact, responsibility to pick up the slack and provide the controls that the child lacks until such time as the child is able to resume self-control. Personal freedom flourishes in a framework of structure. It has been shown that authoritative parents raise the most emotionally resilient children. . . .

Parents need to intervene

Where out of control children are unable to create their own momentum to eat and restore their weight, parents may need to intervene by temporarily taking over the role of symptom manager. Taking charge where the child cannot, parents may provide meals, go to school to meet their child for lunch, offer consequences to the resistant child, etc., much as a nurse would do in a hospital in-patient unit. Younger children typically benefit most from such stringent controls. Parents need to do whatever it takes to nourish the child both physically and emotionally. It is for each family to devise and enact whatever techniques and protocols work best for them.

Parents may converse with the child's therapist to become better educated about eating disorders and the requirements for their child's recovery; they may benefit from conjoint family therapy where they are free to dialogue face to face with their child and family, learning what kinds of changes within themselves might enhance and facilitate changes within the child. Parents might benefit, too, from couples' counseling, where the child's therapist advises and guides them in understanding eating disorders, their child, and their role in recovery. Short of the possibility of the child's committing harm to self or others, therapists need never divulge the child's confidences.

Unless abusive, chaotic, or highly dysfunctional, parents, for the most part, want to assist their child in every way they can; they deserve to be taught how. Managed care is sending severely involved children home from hospitals after six to twelve days to recover under their parent's roof; in most instances, children in outpatient treatment are limited to 45 minutes of psychotherapy a week for a limited number of weeks. It is high time that parents begin to behave as "consumers" of their child's mental health services, learning what to expect and demand of the child's professionals, and how best to work alongside them to facilitate their work and their child's recovery.

Organizations to Contact

The editors have compiled the following list of organizations concerned with the issues debated in this book. The descriptions are derived from materials provided by the organizations. All have publications or information available for interested readers. The list was compiled on the date of publication of the present volume; names, addresses, phone and fax numbers, and e-mail addresses may change. Be aware that many organizations take several weeks or longer to respond to inquiries, so allow as much time as possible.

American Psychiatric Association (APA)
1400 K St. NW, Washington, DC 20005
(202) 682-6000 • fax: (202) 682-6850
e-mail: apa@psych.org • website: www.psych.org

The APA conducts studies on the nature, prevention, and treatment of mental disorders; advocates and helps formulate policies on mental health; disseminates information on psychiatric studies; and promotes psychiatric research and education. The association publishes a monthly journal, the *American Journal of Psychiatry*.

American Psychological Association (APA)
750 First St. NE, Washington, DC 20002-4242
(800) 374-2721 • (202) 336-5500
e-mail: public.affairs@apa.org • website: www.apa.org

The APA advocates for legislation and issues on mental health, helps educate the public about eating disorders, implements the National Eating Disorders Screening Program, and provides information on eating disorders through fact sheets, books, and videos. It produces publications such as the monthly journal *American Psychologist*, the monthly newsletter *APA Monitor*, and the quarterly *Journal of Abnormal Psychology*.

Anorexia Nervosa and Related Eating Disorders (ANRED)
PO Box 5102, Eugene, OR 97405
(541) 344-1144
website: www.anred.com

ANRED provides information on bulimia, anorexia, and other eating disorders, including prevention, treatment, and recovery; offers workshops, training for individuals and professionals, and community education; and produces a monthly newsletter.

Dads and Daughters
PO Box 3458, Duluth, MN 55803
(888) 824-3237 • fax: (218) 722-4058
website: www.dadsanddaughters.org

This organization provides tools to families to strengthen relationships with daughters and emphasizes positive messages that value daughters for who they are and not for how they look.

Harvard Eating Disorders Center (HEDC)
356 Boylston St., Boston, MA 02116
(617) 236-7766 • (888) 236 1188, ext. 100
website: www.hedc.org

The HEDC focuses on research and education on eating disorders; aims to expand knowledge on their detection, prevention, and treatment; promotes the healthy development of women, children, and everyone at risk; and lobbies for health policy initiatives on eating disorders.

National Association of Anorexia Nervosa and Associated Disorders (ANAD)
PO Box 7, Highland Park, IL 60035
(847) 831-3438
e-mail: info@anad.org • website: www.anad.org

ANAD offers hot-line counseling and an international network of support for sufferers and their families; provides referrals to professionals and information, including the publication of a quarterly newsletter; and organizes national conferences and local programs. Services are provided free of charge.

National Eating Disorder Information Centre (NEDIC)
CW 1-211, 200 Elizabeth St., Toronto, ON M5G 2C4 Canada
(416) 340-4156 • fax: (416) 340-4736
e-mail: nedic@uhn.on.ca • website: www.nedic.ca

NEDIC provides information and focuses on the socioeconomic factors that impact womens' health behavior. It promotes healthy lifestyles, advocates for informed choices, publishes a newsletter and a guide for families and friends of sufferers, and sponsors Eating Disorders Awareness Week in Canada.

National Eating Disorders Association (NEDA)
(206) 382-3587
e-mail: info@NationalEatingDisorders.org
website: www.nationaleatingdisorders.org

NEDA is the result of the merging of the Eating Disorders Awareness and Prevention and the American Anorexia Bulimia Association in 2001. It promotes the prevention of eating disorders as well as the access of sufferers to information, care, and support for recovery; supports research on eating disorders; advocates public policies that recognize eating disorders as a serious mental health problem; offers outreach programs and training for schools and universities; sponsors the annual National Eating Disorders Awareness Week; publishes a prevention curriculum for grades four to six; and produces information packets, videos, guides, and other materials.

National Institute of Mental Health (NIMH)
Office of Communications and Public Liaison
(301) 443-4513
e-mail: nimhinfo@nih.gov • website: http://nimh.nih.gov

The NIMH aims to reduce the burden of mental illness through research and education; promotes the better understanding, treatment, and prevention of mental illness, including eating disorders; and produces and distributes publications on eating disorders and other mental health issues.

National Women's Health Information Center
Department of Health and Human Services
(800) 994-9662
website: www.4woman.gov

The center offers information on eating disorders to the general public, health care providers, and school personnel in order to detect eating disorders among adolescents. It also produces and distributes fact sheets and reports and publishes the newsletter *Healthy Women Today.*

Overeaters Anonymous
PO Box 44020, Rio Rancho, NM 87124
(505) 891-2664 • fax: (505) 891-4320
website: www.overeatersanonymous.org

This organization deals with the issues of compulsive eating, provides counseling, and conducts free local meetings.

Rader Programs
26560 Agoura Rd., Suite 108, Calabasas, CA 91302
(800) 841-1515 • fax: (818) 880-3750
e-mail: rader@raderprograms.com • website: www.raderpro.com

The Rader Programs help save the lives of those troubled with eating disorders; has eating treatment programs in California, Illinois, and Oklahoma; and focuses treament on the special needs of individuals.

The Renfrew Center
7700 Refrew Ln., Coconut Creek, FL 33073
(800) 736-3739
website: www.renfrew.org

A women's mental health center with locations in New York, Pennsylvania, Florida, Connecticut, and New Jersey, the Renfrew Center maintains a nationwide referral network; specializes in treating eating disorders, trauma, anxiety, depression, substance abuse, and other women's issues; has outpatient and inpatient care; provides information and educational resources for professionals; and produces audiotapes, books, and videos.

SAFE Alternative (Self Abuse Finally Ends)
7115 W. North Ave., Suite 319, Oak Park, IL 60302
(800) 366-8288

SAFE provides information, support, and treatment programs to those suffering from self-abuse.

Hot Lines

Boys and Girls Town National Hotline
(800) 448-3000 • hearing impaired: (800) 448-1833

Boys and Girls Town provides a twenty-four-hour crisis line for children, parents, and everyone who may have a problem; offers counseling services for immediate concerns; provides referrals for long-term counseling and treatment; and provides services in English, Spanish, and other languages.

(800) THERAPIST Network
(800) 843-7274
This hot line provides referrals to local therapists for any condition.

National Eating Disorders Association
(800) 931-2237
See previous listing for further information.

Websites

Most of the organizations below have websites that provide a wealth of information on eating disorders—their detection, prevention, and treatment. They also indicate various resources, such as seminars, conferences, and national events, as well as fact sheets, pamphlets, and videotapes.

American Dietetic Association (ADA)
216 W. Jackson Blvd., Chicago, IL 60606
(503) 344-0040
website: http://eatright.org

This website contains information on good nutrition as well as results of recent studies on food and nutrition. The ADA sponsors publications, national events, and media/marketing programs.

Anorexia and Bulimia Care (ABC)
website: www.anorexiabulimiacare.co.uk

The ABC provides information on eating disorders and various kinds of resources for sufferers and their families. The organization is based in England.

Anorexia and Bulimia Family Support Group
website: http://users.iafrica.com/r/ro/ronhey/main.htm
e-mail: fsqrsa@iafrica.com

This group's site contains information and support services to sufferers and their families. The organization is based in Johannesburg, South Africa.

Eating Disorder Education Organization
website: www.edeo.org

This organization provides information on eating disorders and support for family and friends of sufferers. The organization is based in Alberta, Canada.

Eating Disorders Coalition (EDC)
website: www.eatingdisorderscoalition.org

The EDC advocates for research, policy, and action. Its website contains information on various initiatives that aim to make eating disorders a public health priority.

Something Fishy Website on Eating Disorders
website: www.something-fishy.org

This website provides information on eating disorders.

Bibliography

Books

Suzanne Abraham and Derek Llewellyn-Jones   *Eating Disorders: The Facts.* New York: Oxford University Press, 1992.

Marlene Boskind-White and William C. White Jr.   *Bulimia/Anorexia: The Binge/Purge Cycle and Self-Starvation.* New York: W.W. Norton, 2000.

Kelly D. Brownell and Christopher G. Fairburn, eds.   *Eating Disorders: A Comprehensive Handbook.* New York: Guilford, 1995.

Liza N. Burby   *Bulimia Nervosa: The Secret Cycle of Bingeing and Purging.* New York: Rosen, 1998.

Janice M. Cauwels   *Bulimia: The Binge-Purge Compulsion.* New York: Doubleday, 1983.

Peggy Claude-Pierre   *The Secret Language of Eating Disorders: The Revolutionary New Approach to Understanding and Curing Anorexia and Bulimia.* New York: Times Books of Random House, 1997.

Peter J. Cooper   *Bulimia Nervosa and Binge-Eating: A Guide to Recovery.* New York: New York University Press, 1995.

Carolyn Costin   *The Eating Disorder Sourcebook: A Comprehensive Guide to the Causes, Treatments, and Prevention of Eating Disorders.* Los Angeles: Lowell House, 1996.

David Goodnough   *Eating Disorders.* Berkeley Heights, NJ: Enslow, 1999.

Bonnie Graves   *Bulimia: Breaking the Cycle of Bingeing and Purging.* Mankato, MN: Capstone, 2000.

Michele E. Siegel, Judith Brisman, and Margot Weinshel   *Surviving an Eating Disorder: Strategies for Family and Friends.* New York: HarperCollins, 1997.

Debbie Stanley   *Understanding Bulimia Nervosa.* New York: Rosen, 1999.

Becky W. Thompson   *A Hunger So Wide and So Deep: American Women Speak Out on Eating Problems.* Minneapolis: University of Minnesota Press, 1994.

Kathryn J. Zerbe   *The Body Betrayed: Women, Eating Disorders, and Treatment.* Washington, DC: American Psychiatric, 1993.

Periodicals

American Psychiatric Association   "Let's Talk Facts About Eating Disorders," publication produced by the APA Joint Commission on Public Affairs and the Division of Public Affairs, revised 1996.

Leslie Berger	"A New Body Politic: Learning to Like the Way We Look," *New York Times*, July 18, 2000.
Edwin Brown	"Bulimia Nervosa: A Modern-Day Medical Mystery," *Medical Update*, vol. 21, no. 3, September 1997.
Susan Chollar	"Eating Disorders: Women at Risk," *Woman's Day*, vol. 60, no. 10, June 3, 1997.
Sandy Fertman	"Real-Life True Story: Bulimia Almost Killed Me," *Teen Magazine*, vol. 41, no. 1, January 1997.
Kay L. Grothaus	"Eating Disorders and Adolescents: An Overview of a Maladaptive Behavior," *Journal of Child and Adolescent Psychiatric Nursing*, vol. 11, no. 4, October 1998.
Carol Krucoff	"Are You Being Led Down the Fitness Path by a Model of Perfection?" *Los Angeles Times*, September 11, 2000.
Lisa Liddane	"Man in the Mirror," *Orange County Register*, August 29, 2001.
Jim McCaffree	"Eating Disorders: All in the Family?" *Journal of the American Dietetic Association*, June 2001.
Beth M. McGilley and Tamara L. Pryor	"Assessment and Treatment of Bulimia Nervosa," *American Family Physician*, vol. 57, no. 11, June 1998.
Merry N. Miller and Andres J. Pumariega	"Culture and Eating Disorders: A Historical and Cross-Cultural Review," *Psychiatry*, vol. 64, no. 2, Summer 2001.
National Institute of Mental Health	"Eating Disorders: Facts About Eating Disorders and the Search for Solutions," NIH publication no. 01-4901, 2001.
New York Times	"Study Links Bulimia to Chemical Malfunction in the Brain," February 16, 1999.
Jennifer Redford	"Are Sexual Abuse and Bulimia Linked?" *Physician Assistant*, vol. 25, no. 3, March 2001.
Sally Squires	"Back to Basics: In Times of Turmoil, Stabilize Your Health with Diet, Sleep, and Exercise," *Washington Post*, September 25, 2001.
Josie L. Tenore	"Challenges in Eating Disorders: Past and Present," *American Family Physician*, vol. 64, no. 3, August 1, 2001.
Emily Wax	"Immigrant Girls Are Starving to Be American, Studies Find," *Washington Post*, March 6, 2000.
Stephen A. Wonderlich et al.	"Relationship of Childhood Sexual Abuse and Eating Disorders," *Journal of the American Academy of Child and Adolescent Psychiatry*, August 1997.

Website

Abigail H. Natenshon	"The Parent Connection in Eating Disorder Recovery: Squeaking the Recovery Wheel." www.empoweredparents.com.

Index

abstinence model, 63–66
acculturation, 8–9, 58
addiction, 63–66
Adler, Virginia, 24
adolescence, 33–36
advertising, 37–38
African Americans, 52
  see also women, African American
Alcoholics Anonymous (AA), 63
alcoholism, 63
Alger, Sharon, 25, 26
American Psychiatric Association, 6, 64
amnesia, 50
Andersen, Arnold E., 29
anorexia nervosa
  cultural changes and, 58
  medical complications from, 24–25
  onset ages of, 12
  shared similarities with bulimia, 7
  signs and symptoms, 28
  see also eating disorders
anxiety disorders, 13
assessment, 15

Beck, Aaron, 62
"biggerexia," 29
bingeing. *See* bulimia; purging
Bloom, Carol, 25
body dysmorphia disorder (BDD), 29
body image
  of adolescents, 35–36
  depression and, 35
  male vs. females on, 33
  women should have a positive, 36–37
Boskind-White, Marlene, 8, 32
boys. *See* men
Brady, Joelle, 24, 26
Bruch, Hilde, 38, 61
bulimia
  cycle of bingeing and, 51–52
  defined, 6
  medical complications from, 24–25
  onset ages of, 12
  prevalence of, 6, 11–12, 43
  psychiatric conditions related to,
    12–13
  sexual abuse connected with, 41–43, 45
  signs and symptoms of, 7, 28, 44
  as solitary, 48
  stages of, 52
  types of bingeing foods for, 6

  see also eating disorders
bulimics
  body habitus of, 44
  older women, 23–24
  treatment of, 26–27
  profile of, 8–9
  testimony of recovering, 17–22
  see also men; women

child abuse, 48
  see also sexual abuse
children, 32–33
Chollar, Susan, 23
cognitive behavioral model (CBT), 62–63
cognitive distortions, 62
Costin, Carolyn, 60
Cousins, Norman, 66

dancers, 39
David, Janet, 25, 26
Demichael, Rodney, 42
depression, 12–13, 35–36
diagnosis, 11, 12
  for African American women, 54–55
  for men, 28–29
dieting
  avoiding painful feelings with, 47
  cycle of bingeing and, 51
  gender socialization and, 48
  by males, 30–31
  as solitary, 48
  women's preoccupation with, 38–39
disease/addiction model, 63–66
disease model, 63–66
drugs vs. food, 51

eating disorders
  as an addiction, 63, 64–65
  buffering pain with, 46–47
  causes of, 11
    acculturation, 8–9, 58
    buffering pain, 46–47, 50–51
    coping mechanism, 8, 47–50
    cultural changes, 8, 58
    cultural expectations, 7, 25, 29–30,
      37
    genetics, 29
    media portrayals of women, 38–39
    personal trauma, 25
    psychological. *See* psychological
      issues

sexual abuse, 7–8, 42, 45
  as counterproductive to effective
    coping, 53
  as increasing in other countries, 59
  as intermittent vs. progressive, 52
  men with. *See* men
  progression of, 51–52
  sexual abuse linked with, 40–41
  see also anorexia nervosa; bulimia;
    women

Fairburn, Christopher, 63
Fallon, Patricia, 25, 27
family. *See* parents
females. *See* girls; women
Fetman, Sandy, 17
food
  vs. alcohol use, 47–48
  buffering pain with, 46–47
  vs. drugs, 51
  junk, 33
  types of bingeing, 6
friends
  intervention from, 20–21
  knowing about bulimic's problem, 18,
    19–20

gender socialization, 47–48
genetics, 29
girls
  body image and, 33
  depression in, 35–36
  stresses of adolescent, 35
  as trained to seek approval, 34–35
  see also women
Glazier, Sheri, 24

Halmi, Katherine, 26
Hamilton, Mary Jane, 23
health care providers, 43–44
Hispanics, 58–59
  see also women
historical amnesia, 50–51
hospitalization, 10, 15, 20

immigrants, 8–9, 49
intervention
  from friends, 20–21
  levels of parental, 69
  need for parental, 69–70
  obstacles to family, 67–68
  see also treatment

Japan, 58
Joseph, Gloria I., 37

Kearney-Cooke, Ann, 53
kibarashi, 58
King, Nancy, 26

Kratina, Karin, 8

lesbians, 49, 50
Lewis, Jill, 37
Liddane, Lisa, 28
low self-esteem. *See* self-esteem
Luciano, Lynne, 30

males. *See* men
McGilley, Beth M., 10
medical complications, 7, 13, 24–25
  for men, 29
  with purging, 14–15
medications, 16, 45
men
  on body image, 33
  cultural expectations of, 33–34
  with eating disorders, 28
  diagnosing, 28–29
  medical complications of, 29
  research on, 29
  treatment of, 31
  weight control by, 30–31
Michaels, Adele, 24
Miller, Merry N., 8
minorities. *See* Hispanics; women,
    African American
mood disorders, 13
Murphy, Terry, 30
muscle dysmorphia, 29

Natenshon, Abigail H., 67
National Eating Disorders Association, 6
Nolen-Hoeksema, Susan, 35

Olivardia, Roberto, 28–29, 30
Overeaters Anonymous (OA), 63–64
overweight people, 32–33

parents
  attitude toward infant's gender, 34
  influence from, 7, 17–18
  need for intervention by, 69–70
  obstacles to involvement by, 67–68
  role in recovery, 69–70
  as suffering from child's eating
    disorders, 26
personality disorders, 13
Pipher, Mary, 35
post-traumatic stress disorder, 43
poverty, 49
preschoolers, 32
prevention and treatment. *See*
    intervention; treatment
Pryor, Tamara L., 10
psychiatric conditions, 12–13
psychodynamic model of treatment,
    61–62
psychological issues, 7

depression, 12–13, 35–36
    health care providers inquiring into,
        44
    of men, 30
    post-traumatic stress disorder, 43
    psychiatric conditions, 12–13
    sexual abuse predisposes victims to, 40
psychotherapy. *See* therapy
Pumariega, Andres J., 8
purging
    cycle of dieting, bingeing and, 51–52
    medical complications with, 14–15
    sexual abusive history and, 41–42
    sneaking around for, 18–19
    see also bulimia

recovery, 21
    parental role in, 69–70
Redford, Jennifer, 7–8, 40
research
    on men with eating disorders, 29
    on sexual abuse/bulimia connection,
        41–43
    on treatments, 16
reverse anorexia, 29
Ries, Dawn, 25
Robinson, Tracy, 53

school, 20
self-esteem, 19, 30, 34
self-induced vomiting. *See* purging
sexual abuse
    as cause of eating disorders, 7–8
    defined, 40
    eating disorders linked to, 40–43, 45
    health care providers inquiring into,
        44
    post-traumatic stress disorder and, 43
    prevalence of, 40
    regaining memories on, 50
Sheppard, Kay, 64–65
Smith, Katharine A., 9
Staffieri, J.R., 32
Steiner-Adair, Catherine, 8
Steinmeyer, Sarah, 30
substance-related disorders, 13
suicide attempts, 44

television, 37
therapy

cognitive behavioral model of, 62–63
    parental involvement in, 69, 70
    psychodynamic model of, 61–62
Thode, Nancy Heade, 25
Thompson, Becky W., 8, 46
Thorpe, Gail, 24, 27
treatment, 9
    clinical perspectives on, 60
    cognitive behavioral model, 62–63
    inpatient, 15–16
    for males, 31
    in a managed care environment,
        10–11
    medication in, 45
    for older women, 26–27
    outcomes of, 45
    psychodynamic model of, 61–62
    resistance to, 56
    twelve-step program as, 63–66
    see also intervention
tryptophan, 9
twelve-step program, 63–66

University of Cincinnati College of
    Medicine, 32

Vandereycken, Walter, 65
vomiting. *See* purging

Walsh, Tim, 63
Ward, Janie Victoria, 53
White, William C., Jr., 8, 32
women
    African American, 8
    case report on, 55–57
    exclusion and, 50–51
    incidence of, 54, 57–58
    underreporting of bulimia in, 57
    cultural expectations of, 37
    extreme self-criticism by, 39
    gender socialization of, 47–48
    immigrant, 49
    negatively portrayed in advertising,
        37–38
    preoccupation with diet, 38–39
    should love body, 36–37
    see also girls

Zerbe, Kathryn J., 8, 24, 54